BRAIN GAMES™ kids

Publications International, Ltd.

Puzzle Constructors: Cihan Altay, Keith Burns, Jeff Cockrell, Julie Cohen, Conceptis Puzzles, Melissa Conner, Don Cook, Jeanette Dall, Harvey Estes, Adrian Fisher, The Grabarchuk Family, Shelly Hazard, David Helton, Helene Hovanec, Steve Karp, Naomi Lipsky, Fred Piscop, Emily Rice, Stephen Ryder, Pete Sarjeant, Andrew Scordellis, Lauren Anne Sharp, Wayne Robert Williams, Alex Willmore

Illustrators: Elizabeth Gerber, Robin Humer, Jay Soto, Jen Torche

Cover Puzzles: Don Cook, Harvey Estes, The Grabarchuk Family, Pete Sarjeant, Lauren Anne Sharp

ISBN-13: 978-1-4508-2072-1
ISBN-10: 1-4508-2072-7

Manufactured in China.

8 7 6 5 4 3 2 1

CONTENTS

IT'S ALL FUN AND GAMES!

Hey Kids! Are you ready to have some fun?

Here's the easiest question in *Brain Games™: Kids:* What's the best way to get the most out of this big book of puzzles? The answer: Read this page first!

We've assembled a huge collection of fun puzzles for you to tackle. You'll find mazes, crosswords, word puzzles, math puzzles—you name it, we've got it! Try to work a variety of different puzzles each time you open this book. That's the best way to give your brain the biggest boost. Other things to keep in mind:

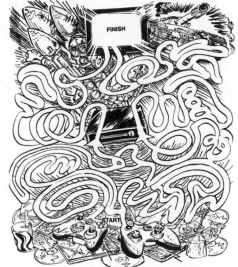

• The puzzles have been sorted into levels, which means you'll find the easiest puzzles at the beginning of the book. If you're really looking for a challenge, head straight to Level 5. Those puzzles are the hardest!

• You can find answers to every puzzle at the back of the book. Just be sure to give each puzzle a fair try before peeking at the answers. You want to be sure to give your brain a full workout before calling for help.

• No matter what puzzle you're working on—whether you solve it in a snap or get hung up on it for what seems like ages—the most important thing to remember is to have fun!

Now you're ready to get started! Every day is a great day for puzzles, so don't wait for a rainy day. (It will just get the pages wet anyway!)

Hello Parents—

The pages of *Brain Games™: Kids* are jammed with an exciting collection of crossword puzzles, word games, mazes, and much more. These puzzles will help your kids give their brains a boost—and the kids will have lots of fun working them! They'll improve their language skills, logical thinking, and analytic reasoning without even realizing it.

We've grouped the puzzles by difficulty level so that you can help guide your child to the puzzles that will suit him or her best. Beginners will love working on the puzzles in Level 1—these easy puzzles are a great way for kids to get a feel for *Brain Games™*. Intermediates will eat up the food for thought in the middle sections (Levels 2 and 3), while advanced puzzlers will love the challenge of the mental marathon of puzzles in Levels 4 and 5. The answers are included at the end of the book, so if they get stuck (or if you do!), just take a peek at the solution to get back on track.

Many educators agree that puzzles and games are among the best ways to engage children in the thinking process. Your mission is to get them started on the journey toward learning. So give them this book and turn them loose on puzzling!

GET YOUR BRAIN GOING

LEVEL I

Weather Terms

Every word listed is contained within the group of letters below. Words can be found in a straight line diagonally, horizontally, or vertically. They may be read either forward or backward.

CLOUD
COLD
FAIR
FOG
FROST
HOT
HUMID
ICE
LIGHTNING
RAIN
SLEET
SNOW
STORM
SUNSHINE
TORNADO
WIND

F	M	D	S	L	E	E	T	F
A	R	L	U	N	T	T	O	A
H	E	O	N	W	O	H	D	I
C	D	C	S	C	O	W	A	R
L	I	G	H	T	N	I	N	G
O	M	O	I	N	I	N	R	O
U	U	O	N	C	A	D	O	F
D	H	R	E	M	R	O	T	S

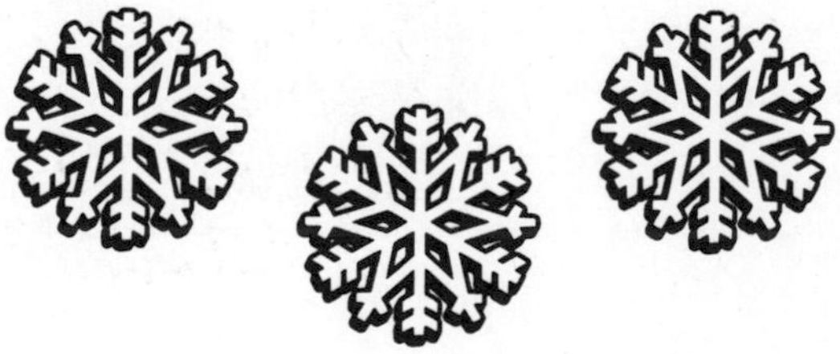

Answers on page 175.

Rhyme Time

Each clue leads to a 2-word answer that rhymes, such as BIG PIG or STABLE TABLE. The numbers in parentheses after the clue give the number of letters in each word. For example, "cookware taken from the oven (3, 3)" would be "hot pot."

1. Heavier hitter (6, 6): _____

2. Recipient of a free evening meal (6, 6): _____

3. Tiny ocean (3, 3): _____

4. Tidier diner (6, 5): _____

5. Has to believe (4, 5): _____

6. Boastful formation in the sky (5, 5): _____

Answers on page 175.

1-2-3

Place the number 1, 2, or 3 in each empty circle. The challenge is to have only these 3 numbers in each connected row and column—no number should repeat. Any combination is allowed.

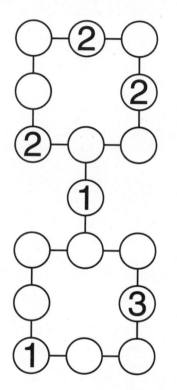

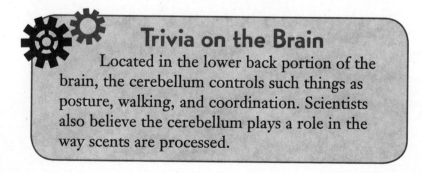

Trivia on the Brain

Located in the lower back portion of the brain, the cerebellum controls such things as posture, walking, and coordination. Scientists also believe the cerebellum plays a role in the way scents are processed.

Answer on page 175.

Honey Bear

Help the bear find a sweet reward at the top of the maze.

Answer on page 175.

Road Trip!

This confused driver is having trouble finding the gas station—and he's running on empty! Follow the arrows to help him find the correct route.

Answer on page 175.

Matching Blots

Find the 2 blots that are identical to each other.

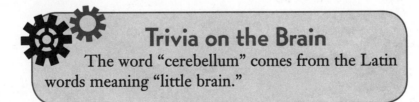

Trivia on the Brain

The word "cerebellum" comes from the Latin words meaning "little brain."

Answer on page 175.

11

Mutations

Look at the 2 words on each line. Someone has not only scrambled the words from the left side to the right, but a letter has been removed as well! Figure out what that letter is and write it in the blank. When you're done, read the letters going down to answer to this riddle: How do bees travel to school?

STOOL ___ LOST

GNAT ___ TAG

BRAID ___ BIRD

BREAD ___ DEAR

MOUSE ___ SOME

ZOOM ___ MOO

GAZE ___ AGE

Typewriter Error

The names of two animals have been accidentally typed on top of each other. Can you decipher what they are?

Answers on page 175.

Decoder

Use the code below to reveal the answer to this riddle: Where did the golf gear go after a long day?

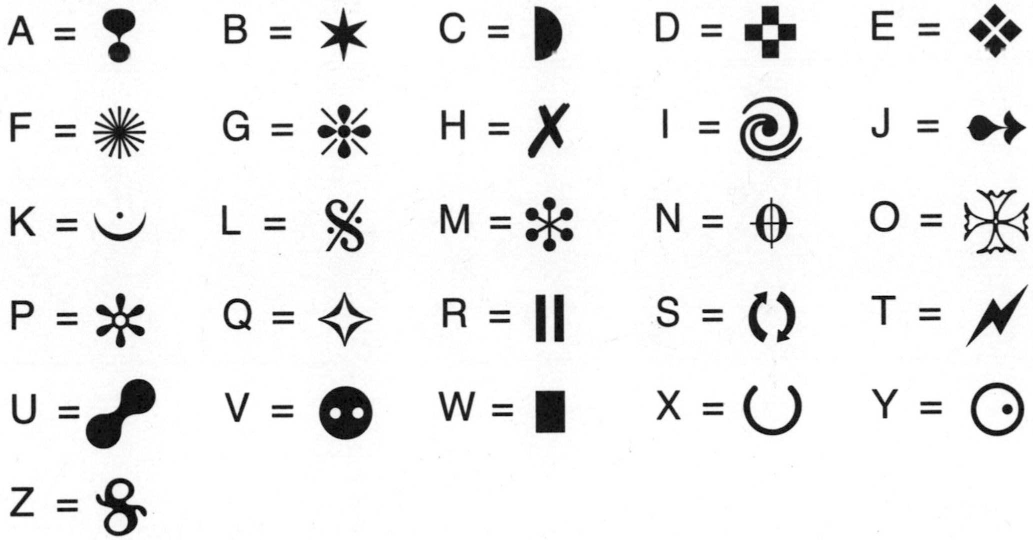

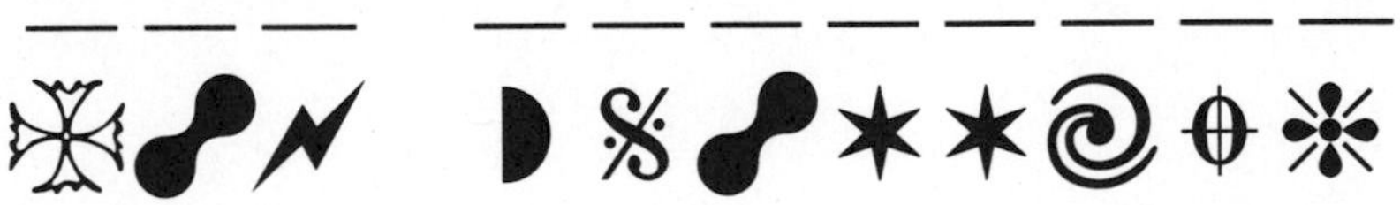

A = ⬤ B = ✶ C = ◗ D = ✚ E = ◈

F = ✺ G = ✿ H = ✗ I = ◎ J = ➤

K = ◡ L = ✗ M = ✴ N = ⊕ O = ✾

P = ✳ Q = ◇ R = ‖ S = ◖◗ T = ⚡

U = ⬗ V = ◎ W = ◼ X = ◡ Y = ☉

Z = ✇

___ ___ ___   ___ ___ ___ ___ ___ ___ ___ ___

✾ ⬗ ⚡   ◗ ✗ ⬗ ✶ ✶ ◎ ⊕ ✳

Answer on page 175.

13

Flower Growth

Which of these flowers has the longest stem?

Word Ladder

Can you change just one letter on each line to transform the top word to the bottom word? Don't change the order of the letters, and make sure you have a common English word at each step.

WEE

_____

_____

BIG

Answers on page 175.

Find the Blocks

Find the shapes at the right in the grid as many times as listed. The shapes must be facing the same direction as the examples.

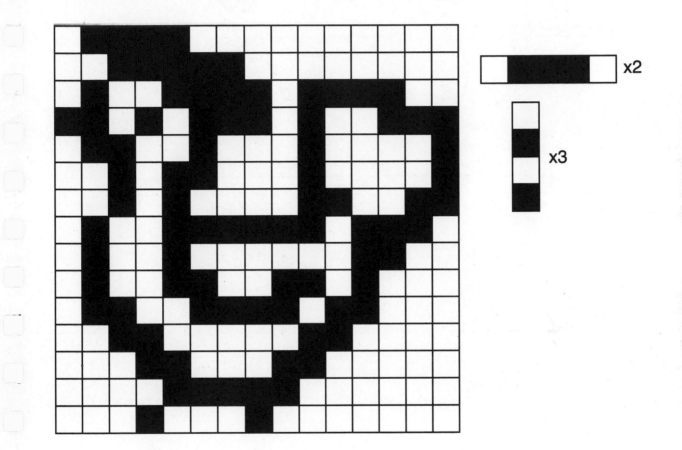

Answer on page 176.

15

Treasure Chests

How many treasure chests can you find in this dragon scene?

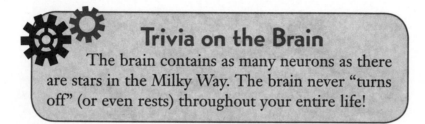

Trivia on the Brain

The brain contains as many neurons as there are stars in the Milky Way. The brain never "turns off" (or even rests) throughout your entire life!

Answer on page 176.

Number Code: Any Questions?

First, solve each of the arithmetic problems. Then, find the corresponding letter in the number code at right. Write the letter for that number on the second dash. Reading down the column of letters will reveal the hidden words.

1. $5 + 10 =$ ___ ___

   $3 + 9 =$ ___ ___

   $4 + 4 =$ ___ ___

2. $9 + 6 =$ ___ ___

   $7 + 5 =$ ___ ___

   $4 + 3 =$ ___ ___

   $6 + 3 =$ ___ ___

3. $8 + 7 =$ ___ ___

  $11 + 1 =$ ___ ___

   $6 + 12 =$ ___ ___

   $3 + 2 =$ ___ ___

4. $4 + 11 =$ ___ ___

   $2 + 10 =$ ___ ___

   $7 + 11 =$ ___ ___

   $2 + 4 =$ ___ ___

  $15 + 3 =$ ___ ___

5. $12 + 3 =$ ___ ___

   $8 + 4 =$ ___ ___

   $9 + 7 =$ ___ ___

CODE

1. K	14. X
2. L	15. W
3. J	16. Y
4. I	17. P
5. N	18. E
6. R	19. C
7. A	20. V
8. O	21. Q
9. T	22. G
10. Z	23. B
11. U	24. S
12. H	25. M
13. D	26. F

Answers on page 176.

Picture This

Copy the picture in each numbered square into the same numbered square in the grid to reveal a picture pointing you in the right direction.

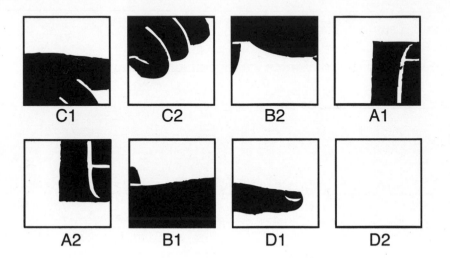

C1   C2   B2   A1

A2   B1   D1   D2

	A	B	C	D
1				
2				

Answer on page 176.

Riddle Scramble

Use the scrambled words to solve each of the clues below. Once you've done that, unscramble the letters found in the boxes to solve this riddle: I love to swim, but I can't drown. What am I?

1. I'm used in the sun and I'm lots of _____.

2. I'm able to stay on top of the water without sinking because I know how to _____.

3. People can use me in a lake or an _____.

4. I'm hollow, and need to be full of _____ to work.

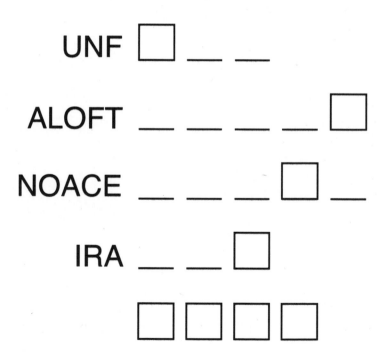

Answers on page 176.

19

Flippy Numbers

Below is an incorrect equation. Can you swap 2 of the number cards to get a correct equation?

$$1 + 2 + 3 = 5 + 7$$

Paper Fold

What fruit is written on this folded paper?

Answers on page 176.

Find the Mice

There are 8 mice hiding in this kitchen. Can you find them all?

Answer on page 176.

Theme Park

This "ride" has a theme, but we can't tell you what it is. Place all the words in the boxes below—when you do, read the word created in the outlined boxes, from top to bottom, to reveal what the theme is.

ICE CREAM   SURPRISE

THEME   PARTY

CAKE   FRIENDS

is melting

special effects

with candles

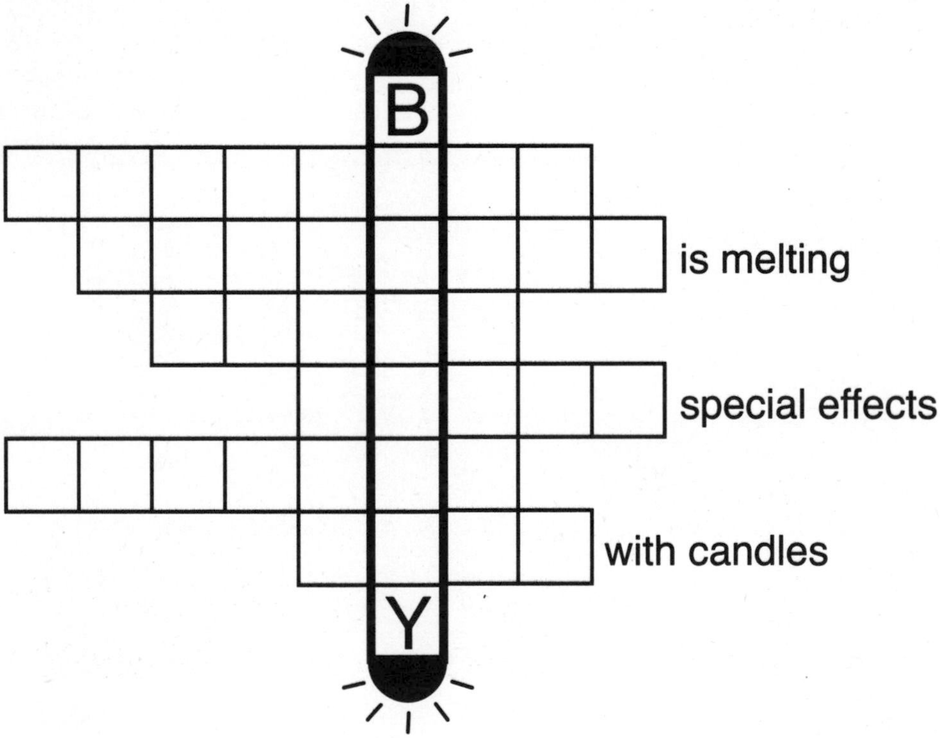

Answer on page 176.

Vex-a-Gon

Place the numbers 1 through 6 into the triangles of each hexagon. The numbers may be in any order, but they do not repeat within each hexagon shape (6-sided shape around each black dot).

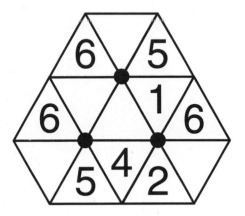

Paper Fold

What sport is written on this folded paper?

Answers on page 177.

Crazy Maze

Can you find your way through this tangled maze?

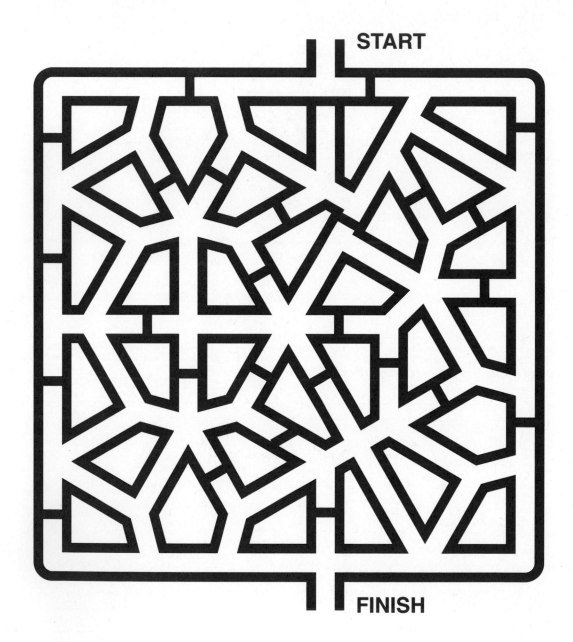

Answer on page 177.

Polyshapes

Which shape does not belong in this sequence?

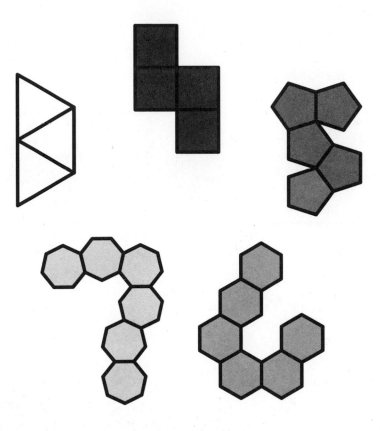

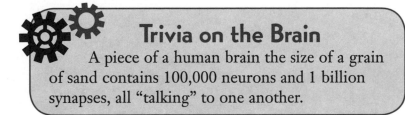

Trivia on the Brain

A piece of a human brain the size of a grain of sand contains 100,000 neurons and 1 billion synapses, all "talking" to one another.

Answer on page 177.

Marty the Moose

Marty has invited some friends to dinner. Only those friends with shapes matching the party decorations on Marty's antlers may come. How many are coming to dinner?

Answer on page 177.

Word Ladder

Can you change just one letter on each line to transform the top word to the bottom word? Don't change the order of the letters, and make sure you have a common English word at each step.

EASY

_____ the sun rises from this direction

_____ the doctor puts a broken leg in this

_____ you push this in the grocery store

_____ you send this to a sick friend

HARD

Answer on page 177.

Chain Words

Place 3 letters in the middle squares that will complete one word and start another. For example, TAR would complete GUI - TAR - GET.

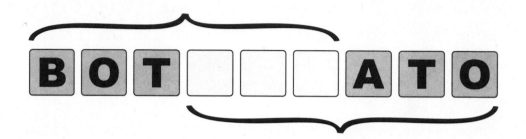

Word Math

This puzzle works exactly like a regular math problem, but instead of using numbers in the equation you use letters. First, fill in the blanks with the proper name for each picture. Then solve the equation.

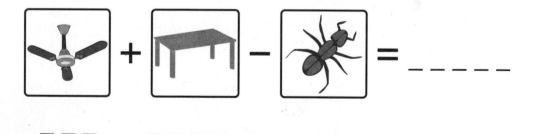

Answers on page 177.

Report Card

Billy's parents were very impressed with Billy's report card this quarter. One subject was still a little low, but overall there was vast improvement in his grades from the first quarter of the year. In celebration of his much-improved report card, Billy got a treat—he could take a friend to the water park that weekend! Determine the grade Billy got in each subject (he got 2 A's, 2 B's, and one C).

1. His English grade is better than his science grade.

2. He didn't get an A in social studies.

3. He did better in science than he did in Spanish.

4. He got an A in math.

	A	A	B	B	C
English					
Math					
Science					
Social Studies					
Spanish					

Answer on page 177.

Number Anagram

Can you come up with 6 different words using only the letters in NUMBER? Letters can be used more than once.

____ ____ ____ ____

____ ____

____ ____ ____

____ ____ ____ ____

____ ____ ____

____ ____

Paper Fold

What article of clothing is written on this folded paper?

Answers on page 177.

G Is for Ghost!

Can you find the 15 ghosts and skeletons in this illustration? As a bonus, see if you can spot the mummies as well!

Answers on page 177.

Aye, Matey!

ACROSS

1. Good friend
4. Family dog or cat
7. Health resort
10. How old you are
11. "_____ Baba and the Forty Thieves"
12. Hearing organ
13. Jolly _____ (pirate flag)
15. Walking the _____ (pirate punishment)
17. Senior: abbr.
18. "_____ what?" ("Who cares?")
19. Animal often called a buffalo
22. Captain Hook's pirate assistant
26. Place for a computer mouse
27. Actor Hanks or Cruise
29. Money-dispensing machine: abbr.
30. Pirate's drink
32. Goes right or left
34. Extended play: abbr.
36. _____ and fro
37. _____ and crossbones (symbol on a pirate flag)
40. Song beginning, for short
44. _____ and hers
45. Have possession of
47. Compete in a race
48. Number of eyes a cyclops has
49. "My _____ or the highway!"
50. Mornings: abbr.

DOWN

1. Golf score to shoot for
2. Long _____ (in the past)
3. Peg _____ (pirate's artificial limb)
4. Bird on a pirate's shoulder
5. _____ Paso, Texas
6. Money left for the waitstaff
7. _____ dog (another name for a pirate)
8. "Peter _____" (movie featuring the pirate Captain Hook)
9. Noah's _____
14. The letter S, spelled out
16. _____ Angeles, California
19. Salad _____ (self-serve part of a restaurant)
20. Words spoken by a bride and groom
21. "She loves me . . . she loves me _____"
23. "_____ overboard!" (yell from a pirate ship)
24. Extraterrestrials: abbr.
25. The letter "M," spelled out
26. "Parental Guidance Recommended" movie rating
28. Rebellion on a pirate ship
31. Gooey hair product
33. Movie director _____ Howard
35. Farm tool pulled by oxen
37. TV channel Showtime, for short

38. Relatives
39. "It's no _____!" (quitter's words)
41. "_____-la-la"
42. "Yo-ho-ho and a bottle of _____"
    (words from a pirate song)

43. Roll-_____ (some deodorants)
46. Washington state: abbr.

Answers on page 177.

33

Nice Trike

Which tricycle is the mirror image of the one in the box?

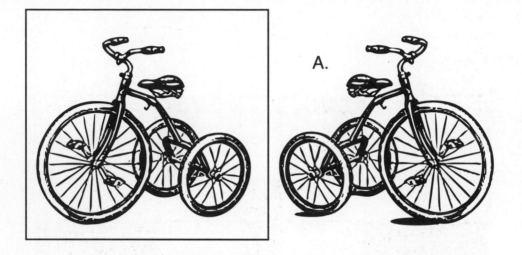

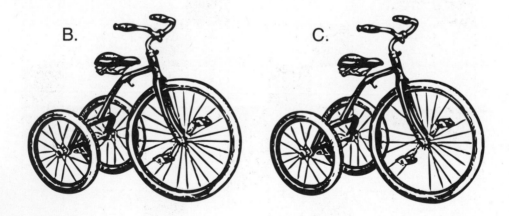

Answer on page 178.

Fit It

Figure out the names for each of the modes of transportation below, then fit those names into the crossword grid.

ACROSS

DOWN

Answer on page 178.

Bugs!

There are a lot of bugs on display here. Which one bug appears most in this collection?

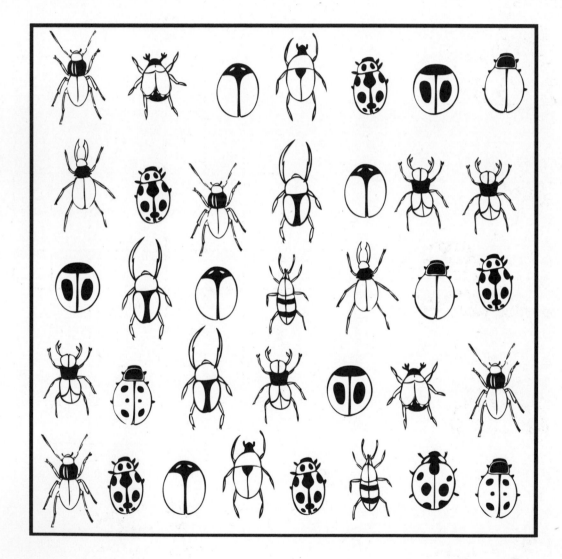

Answer on page 178.

Theme Park

This "ride" has a theme, but we can't tell you what it is. Place all the words in the boxes below. When you do, read the word created in the outlined boxes, from top to bottom, to reveal what the theme is. Here's a hint: You don't have to go here on Saturday.

REPORT   HOMEWORK

HOLIDAY   COMPUTERS

SPORTS   BUS STOP

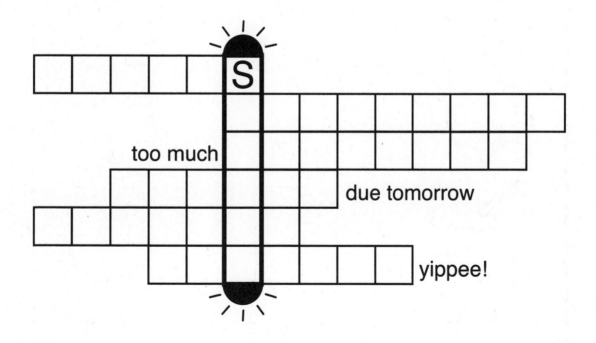

Answer on page 178.

37

Brave Knights

Each one of these knights is missing one detail present in the others. Can you spot all 6?

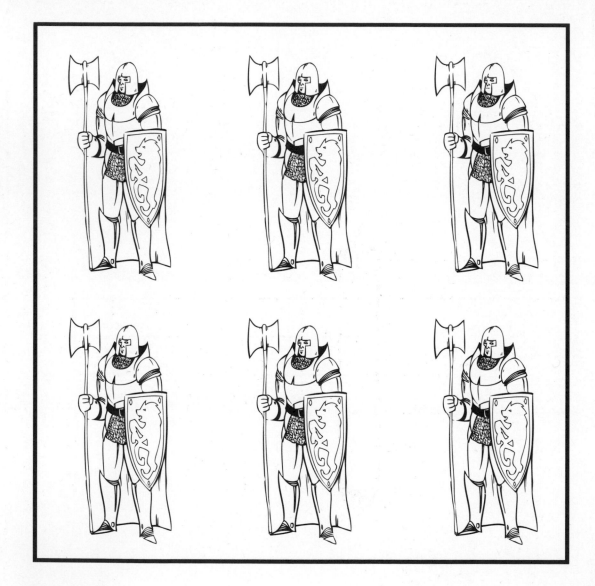

Answers on page 178.

Home Sweet Home

Watch out for black holes as you help this alien return to his home planet.

Answer on page 178.

BUILD YOUR MENTAL MUSCLE

At the Ball

These ladies have all turned up for the grand ball but...UH OH! Two of them are dressed the same. Can you spot which two girls are dressed exactly the same?

Answer on page 178.

1-2-3

Place the number 1, 2, or 3 in each empty circle. The challenge is to have only these 3 numbers in each connected row and column—no number should repeat. Any combination is allowed.

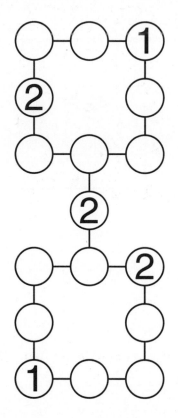

Trivia on the Brain

Believe it or not, thinking takes energy. More blood flows to the brain when we think hard, and that takes energy from elsewhere in our bodies.

Answer on page 178.

Flower Growth

Which of these flowers has the longest stem?

Chain Words

Place 3 letters in the middle squares that will complete one word and start another. For example, TAR would complete GUI - TAR - GET.

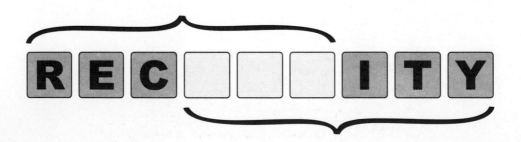

Answers on page 178.

Rhyme Time

Each clue leads to a 2-word answer that rhymes, such as BIG PIG or STABLE TABLE. The numbers in parentheses after the clue give the number of letters in each word. For example, "cookware taken from the oven (3, 3)" would be "hot pot."

1. More ancient giant rock (5, 7). _____

2. Argue faster (6, 7): _____

3. Lawrence's red fruit (6, 8): _____

4. Chocolate-colored dress (5, 4): _____

5. Peanut-butter partner with a foul odor (6, 5): _____

6. Recently purchased footwear (3, 4): _____

7. Better Rollerblader (7, 6): _____

8. Purchase a classic American dessert (3, 3): _____

9. Device for weighing postal materials (4, 5): _____

Trivia on the Brain

Research has shown that the newest cells in your brain can be taught more easily than the more mature cells.

Answers on page 178.

School Days

Every word listed is contained within the group of letters below. Words can be found in a straight line diagonally, horizontally, or vertically. They may be read either forward or backward.

ART

BOOKS

BUS

CHAIR

DESK

EASEL

GEOGRAPHY

LIBRARY

MATH

MUSIC

PRINCIPAL

READING

RECESS

SPELLING

STUDENT

TEACHER

WRITING

```
G N I L L E P S R B
T E A C H E R K Z U
M Y O R B L I O L S
A U L G N E N O I S
T H S N R S C B B T
H Z Z I Q A I W R U
K S E D C E P A A D
L C H A I R A H R E
R E C E S S L R Y N
C H W R I T I N G T
```

Answers on page 179.

Mutations

Look at the 2 words on each line. Someone has not only scrambled the words from the left side to the right, but a letter has been removed as well! Figure out what that letter is and write it in the blank. When you're done, read the letters going down to answer this riddle: What large cat should you never play cards with?

AWAKE ___ WEAK

MUCH ___ HUM

GATHER ___ GREAT

YELLOW ___ LOWLY

LODGE ___ GOLD

SENATOR ___ REASON

MARINE ___ MINER

SHOWER ___ WORSE

Answers on page 179.

Riddle in the Middle

Use the clues to complete the 5-letter answers, starting at the top and working your way down. When finished, read the letters in the squares with the thick boxes, from top to bottom, to reveal the answer to the riddle below.

What word becomes smaller when you add two letters to it?

1. Underdog victory

   U [ ] [ ] [ ] T

2. Knight's outfit

   A [ ] [ ] [ ] R

3. Railroad vehicle

   T [ ] [ ] [ ] N

4. Tummy

   B [ ] [ ] [ ] Y

5. Use crayons

   C [ ] [ ] [ ] R

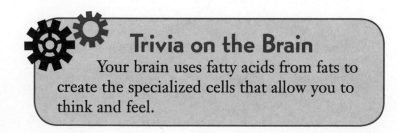

Trivia on the Brain

Your brain uses fatty acids from fats to create the specialized cells that allow you to think and feel.

Answers on page 179.

Matching Blots

Find the 2 blots that are identical to each other.

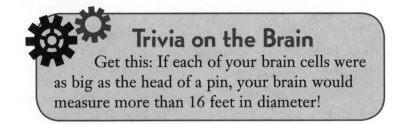

Trivia on the Brain

Get this: If each of your brain cells were as big as the head of a pin, your brain would measure more than 16 feet in diameter!

Answer on page 179.

Find the Blocks

Find the shape at the right in the grid as many times as listed. The shapes must be facing the same direction as the example.

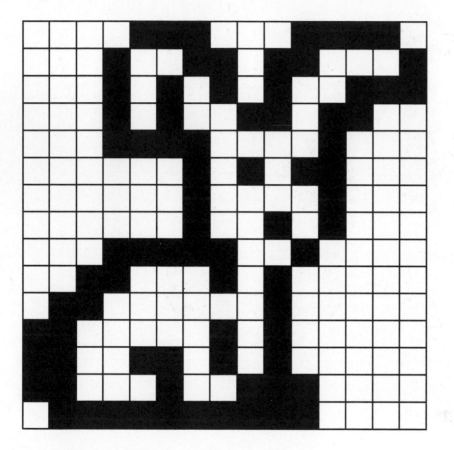

 x4

Answer on page 179.

Vex-a-Gon

Place the numbers 1 through 6 into the triangles of each hexagon. The numbers may be in any order, but they do not repeat within each hexagon shape (6-sided shape around each black dot).

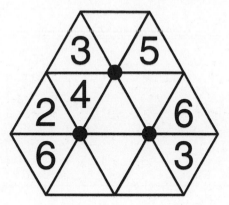

Word Ladder

Can you change just one letter on each line to transform the top word to the bottom word? Don't change the order of the letters, and make sure you have a common English word at each step.

BAIT

_____ you pay this to get out of jail

_____ what water does at 212 degrees Fahrenheit

_____ a spiral structure

_____ relatively cold

_____ prepare food for dinner

HOOK

Answers on page 179.

Crosspic

Looks like someone put pictures in this puzzle where there are supposed to be words! See if you can fill in the grid by writing the word—one letter for each box—that names each of the pictures. Words run across and down.

Answers on page 179.

Chain Words

Place 3 letters in the middle squares that will complete one word and start another. For example, TAR would complete GUI - TAR - GET.

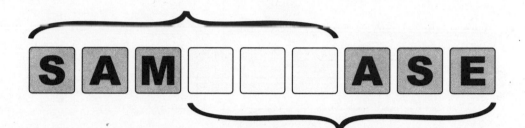

Flippy Numbers

Below is an incorrect equation. Can you swap 2 of the number cards to get a correct equation?

$$3 \times 9 = 46$$

Answers on page 179.

51

Picture This

Copy the picture in each numbered square into the same numbered square in the grid to reveal some things you'd find in a classroom.

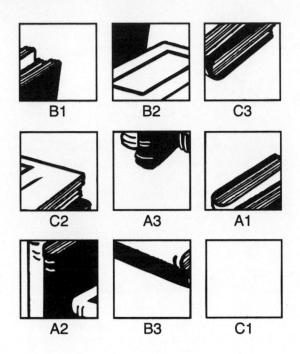

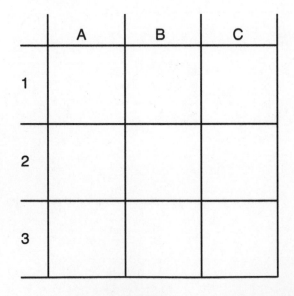

Answer on page 179.

Decoder

Dr. Stitchemup wrote down the tools he needs for surgery on the same paper as his grocery list. The nurse can't read his sloppy handwriting. Can you help her identify which items are for surgery? Use the code below to decipher Dr. Stitchemup's writing. When you finish, check off the boxes for the surgical items.

☐ K⌒IFE

☐ B ᚱ E ◊ D

☐ NE E ⊐ LE

☐ C U EE S E

☐ THR E ◊ ⊐

☐ A Φ Φ LES

☐ M I L K

☐ M ◊ S K

A = ◊   B = ᚱ   C = ᚏ   D = ⊐   E = ⋏

F = ᚎ   G = φ   H = ⊶   I = ǂ   J = ✝

K = ⋔   L = λ   M = ⋈   N = ⌒   O = ȼ

P = Φ   Q = ᛋ   R = ᚱ   S = ᛅ   T = ↓

U = ᴗ   V = ↲   W = ⋉   X = ϖ   Y = ⋋

Z = ᚋ

Answers on page 179.

Riddle Scramble

Use the scrambled words to solve each of the clues below. Once you've done that, unscramble the letters found in the boxes to solve this riddle: I leave hair everywhere I go. What am I?

1. I do this to get under a fence.

2. When my tail does this, it means I like you.

3. My _____ is often wet and cold.

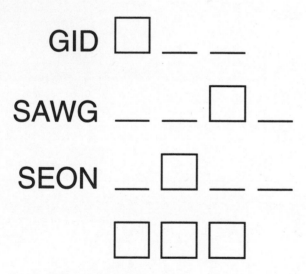

GID ☐ __ __

SAWG __ __ ☐ __

SEON __ ☐ __ __

☐ ☐ ☐

Answers on page 179.

Fit It

Figure out the names for each of the images below, then fit those names into the crossword grid.

ACROSS

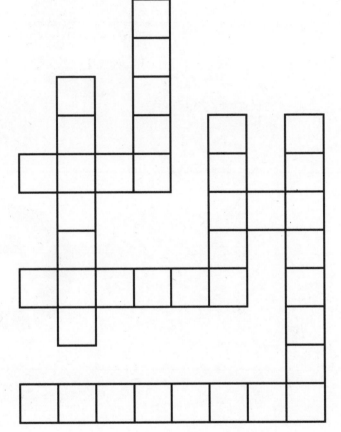

DOWN

Answer on page 180.

Circled Digits

Which shape does not properly follow this sequence?

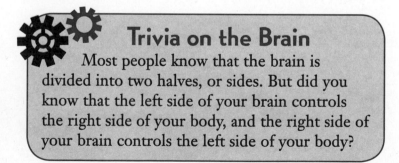

Trivia on the Brain

Most people know that the brain is divided into two halves, or sides. But did you know that the left side of your brain controls the right side of your body, and the right side of your brain controls the left side of your body?

Answers on page 180.

Word Math

This puzzle works exactly like a regular math problem, but instead of using numbers in the equation you use letters. First, fill in the blanks with the proper name for each picture. Then solve the equation.

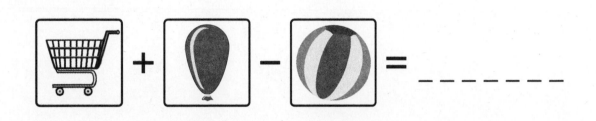

= _ _ _ _ _ _ _

_ _ _ _   _ _ _ _ _ _   _ _ _ _

Paper Fold

What country is written on this folded paper?

Answers on page 180.

H Is for House

Find the 20 hidden objects in the scene below.

HAIR	HELMET	HORSE
HAMBURGER	HEN	HOT DOG
HAMMOCK	HIPPOPOTAMUS	HOT TUB
HAT	HOG	HOURGLASS
HEADPHONES	HOLE	HULA HOOP
HEART	HONEY	HULA SKIRT
HEDGES	HOOD	

Answer on page 180.

Theme Park

This "ride" has a theme, but we can't tell you what it is. Place all the words in the boxes below—when you do, read the word created in the outlined boxes, from top to bottom, to reveal what the theme is.

HISTORY   CHALKBOARD

ENGLISH   WEBSITE

ALGEBRA   CHEMISTRY

PHYSICS

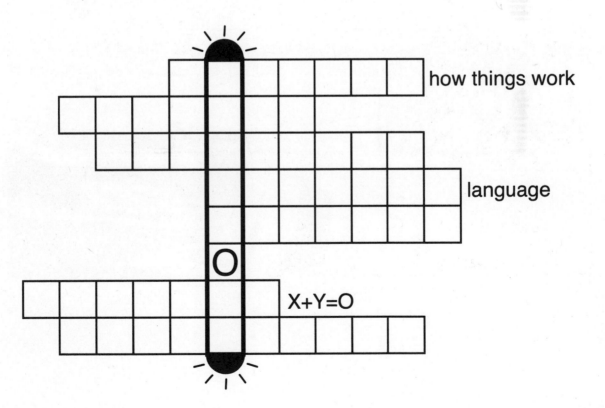

how things work

language

$X+Y=O$

Answer on page 180.

Peter the Polar Bear

Peter has caught 4 fish to give to his friends. Only those friends wearing glasses will get a fish. Can you find them?

Answer on page 180.

Bird Jumbles

Unscramble the letters to spell the names of 8 kinds of birds. The boxed letters will give you the answer to this riddle:

Q: What happens to a duck when he flies upside down?

A: He _____ !

AIULQ

☐ _ _ I _

LSLEUAG

S _ _ _ _ ☐ _ L

LGEAE

_ ☐ G _ _

WOCR

☐ _ _ _

EKAETPAR

P _ _ _ _ ☐ _ E _

RTISCHO

O ☐ _ R _ _ _

CAUNOT

T _ ☐ _ _ N

NIUNEPG

☐ _ _ G _ _ N

Answers on page 180.

61

Number Code: J-Boys

First, solve each of the arithmetic problems. Then, find the corresponding letter in the number code at right. Write the letter for that number on the second dash. Reading down the column of letters will reveal the hidden words.

1. 15 + 1 − 12 = __ __

   3 + 7 − 8 = __ __

   7 + 1 − 5 = __ __

  16 + 4 − 11 = __ __

2. 18 + 1 − 15 = __ __

   2 + 13 − 8 = __ __

  22 + 2 − 19 = __ __

   4 + 7 − 10 = __ __

  13 + 12 − 2 = __ __

3. 17 + 7 − 20 = __ __

  11 + 8 − 18 = __ __

  15 + 1 − 11 = __ __

   9 + 3 − 11 = __ __

   9 + 4 − 7 = __ __

  12 + 9 − 10 = __ __

4. 13 + 8 − 17 = __ __

  10 + 1 − 9 = __ __

  27 + 4 − 21 = __ __

   5 + 6 − 8 = __ __

   6 + 7 − 5 = __ __

  18 + 5 − 16 = __ __

5. 5 + 5 − 6 = __ __

   7 + 9 − 14 = __ __

  24 + 5 − 20 = __ __

  13 + 8 − 14 = __ __

  17 + 5 − 10 = __ __

   8 + 8 − 13 = __ __

   6 + 2 − 1 = __ __

   8 + 8 − 7 = __ __

CODE

1. E	14. X
2. O	15. W
3. H	16. V
4. J	17. Q
5. R	18. G
6. M	19. L
7. A	20. I
8. U	21. P
9. N	22. C
10. S	23. D
11. Y	24. F
12. T	25. B
13. Z	26. K

Answers on page 180.

On the Bus

Five friends get on the same bus every morning to go to school. While they're great friends and have been for years, each one lives on a different street and gets on the bus at a different stop. Determine the street name where each friend gets on the bus and the order in which they are picked up in the morning.

1. Sara isn't the first on the bus. Marcia lives on a Street not a Road.

2. Patti is the fourth to be picked up.

3. Emily doesn't live on East Street.

4. The girl who gets on the bus first lives on West Street.

5. Sara doesn't live on South Road.

6. The friend who lives on North Road is picked up before Sara but after Marcia.

Name	Street	Order
Emily		
Marcia		
Patti		
Sara		

	East Street	North Road	South Road	West Street	1st	2nd	3rd	4th
Emily								
Marcia								
Patti								
Sara								
1st								
2nd								
3rd								
4th								

Answer on page 181.

Here Be Treasure!

There's a bounty of differences between these 2 scenes. Can you spot all 8, matey?

Answers on page 181.

Game Time!

Can you zap your way through the twists and turns of this maze?

Answer on page 181.

Getting There

ACROSS

1. Transportation to school
4. "Friend or _____?"
7. Transportation that's hailed on city streets
10. "A penny saved _____ penny earned"
11. Et cetera: abbr.
12. President Lincoln, for short
13. Hiawatha's transportation
15. Cowboy's transportation
17. Road: abbr.
18. "Wanna make something _____ it?"
19. Covered _____ (pioneer transportation)
22. Cost of riding a bus or taxi
26. Tree fluid
27. Neither here _____ there
29. Moving company's transportation
30. It may be expressed in square miles
32. The silent member of the Seven Dwarfs
34. Los Angeles: abbr.
36. Connecticut: abbr.
37. Transportation that runs on rails
40. Eskimo's water transportation
44. Farm animal that eats slop
45. Easter egg coloring
47. Ginger _____ (soft drink)
48. Female sheep
49. "Ready, _____, go!"
50. Mother's Day month

DOWN

1. Popular brand of pen
2. Our country: abbr.
3. _____ Diego, California
4. Get nourishment from (2 wds.)
5. Overtime: abbr.
6. Sound bounceback, in a cave
7. Family transportation
8. Tummy muscles, for short
9. Honey-making insect
14. Organization: abbr.
16. "They're _____!" (racetrack cry)
19. Simple card game for 2 players
20. Gorilla or chimp
21. Say "yes" by moving your head
23. Avenue: abbr.
24. Bit of sunshine
25. _____ route (on the way)
26. South America: abbr.
28. Spaceman's transportation
31. "_____ Baba and the Forty Thieves"
33. Parent-teacher association: abbr.
35. "No ifs, _____, or buts!"
37. Fill in _____ blank
38. Use oars
39. How old you are
41. Orange Thanksgiving vegetable
42. Chicken _____ king
43. Item needed to open a lock
46. "Hear _____!" (words before a public announcement, once)

1	2	3	■	4	5	6	■	7	8	9
10			■	11			■	12		
13			14		■	15	16			
■	■	■	17		■	18		■	■	■
■	19	20			21	■	22	23	24	25
26			■	27		28	■	29		■
30		31	■	32		33			■	■
■	■	34	35	■	36		■	■	■	■
37	38	39		■	■	40		41	42	43
44			■	45	46		■	47		
48			■	49			■	50		

Answers on page 181.

Waterspout

This maze is a splash! Can you find the water's slippery path to the cup?

Answer on page 181.

Theme Park

This "ride" has a theme, but we can't tell you what it is. Place all the words in the boxes below—when you do, read the word created in the outlined boxes, from top to bottom, to reveal what the theme is. Here's a hint: It's where you go camping.

BIRCH   MOSS

LEAF   MAPLE

STUMP   OAK

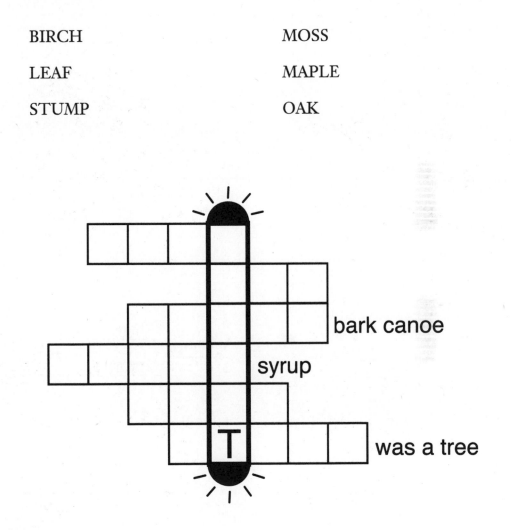

bark canoe

syrup

was a tree

Answer on page 181.

Rose Red

Which roses are the mirror image of the ones in the box?

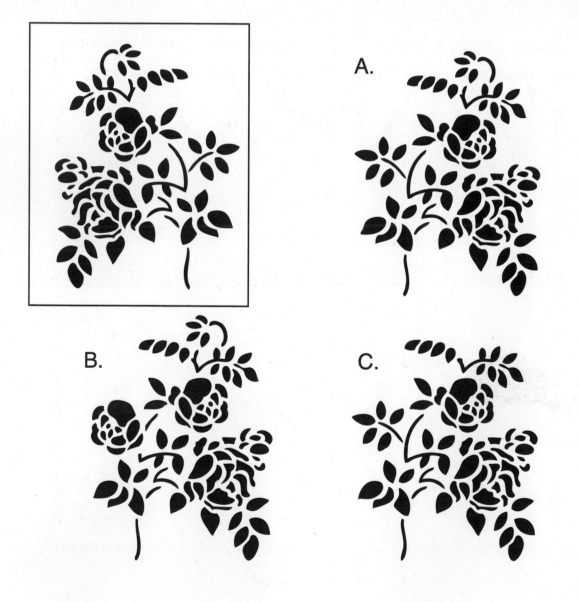

A.

B.

C.

Answer on page 181.

Crazy Maze

Can you find your way through this tangled maze?

Answer on page 181.

NOW YOUR MIND IS MOVING

1-2-3

Place the number 1, 2, or 3 in each empty circle. The challenge is to have only these 3 numbers in each connected row and column—no number should repeat. Any combination is allowed.

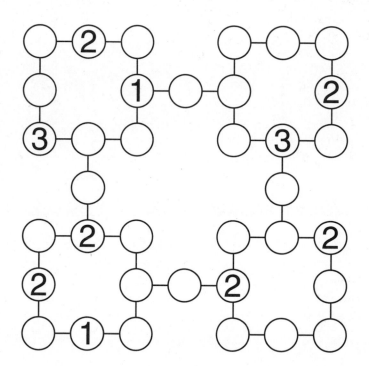

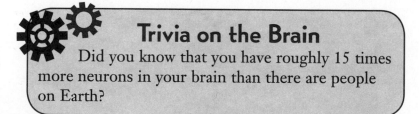

Trivia on the Brain

Did you know that you have roughly 15 times more neurons in your brain than there are people on Earth?

Answer on page 182.

Matching Blots

Find the 2 blots that are identical to each other.

Answer on page 182.

Vex-a-Gon

Place the numbers 1 through 6 into the triangles of each hexagon. The numbers may be in any order, but they do not repeat within each hexagon shape (6-sided shape around each black dot).

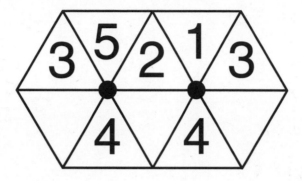

Typewriter Error

Two kitchen items have been accidentally typed on top of each other. Can you decipher what they are?

Answers on page 182.

Ducks

Help make way for these ducklings by guiding them through the maze back to their mom.

Answer on page 182.

Fit It

Figure out the names for each of the animals below, then fit those names into the crossword grid.

ACROSS

DOWN

Answer on page 182.

Flower Growth

Which of these flowers has the longest stem?

Word Ladder

Can you change just one letter on each line to transform the top word to the bottom word? Don't change the order of the letters, and make sure you have a common English word at each step.

SICK

_____

_____

_____

WELL

Answers on page 182.

Find the Blocks

Find the shape at the right in the grid as many times as listed. The shapes must be facing the same direction as the example.

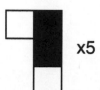 x5

Answer on page 182.

Numbers

Every word listed is contained within the group of letters below. Words can be found in a straight line diagonally, horizontally, or vertically. They may be read either forward or backward.

```
M U S D G H T H I R T Y
A C Y D E R D N U H W W
Z L D N A S U O H T E M
N E E T F I F I W L L W
I L F I T X L L S T V S
N G O E G T Q L O N E T
E E R H T H Y I T V V J
M X T I T T M E R I I
O O Y I F C N N S E F E
B Q H I X P E L E V E N
C M F F F Y W J K O D B
O J T H I R T E E N I Z
```

EIGHT	HUNDRED	THIRTEEN
ELEVEN	MILLION	THIRTY
FIFTEEN	NINE	THOUSAND
FIFTY	ONE	THREE
FIVE	SEVEN	TWELVE
FORTY	SIX	TWENTY
FOUR	TEN	TWO

Answers on page 182.

Rhyme Time

Each clue leads to a 2-word answer that rhymes, such as BIG PIG or STABLE TABLE. The numbers in parentheses after the clue give the number of letters in each word. For example, "cookware taken from the oven (3, 3)" would be "hot pot."

1. Dark-colored ramshackle house (5, 5): _____

2. Enemy of swamp predators (5, 5): _____

3. Builds flat floating vessels (6, 5): _____

4. Divided cherry seed (5, 3): _____

5. Rapid selection (5, 4): _____

6. Farthest west (5, 4): _____

7. Small tiff (6, 5): _____

8. Admirable quality (5, 5): _____

9. Footwear for a crafty woodland creature (3, 5): _____

10. Embrace from an insect (3, 3): _____

11. Long-necked bird running wild (5, 5): _____

12. Entire dish for cereal or soup (5, 4): _____

Answers on page 182.

Clear as Day

Which window washer is the mirror image of the one in the box?

A.

B.

C.

D.

Answer on page 182.

Riddle in the Middle

Use the clues to complete the 5-letter answers, starting at the top and working your way down. When finished, read the letters in the squares with the thick boxes, from top to bottom, to reveal the answer to the riddle below.

What building in Chicago has more stories than the Willis Tower?

1. Distance measures

| M | | | | S |

2. Not moving

| S | | | | L |

3. Book of pictures

| A | | | | M |

4. "_____ Blind Mice"

| T | | | | E |

5. Purple fruit

| G | | | | E |

6. Small sheet of paper

| S | | | | P |

7. Of a king

| R | | | | L |

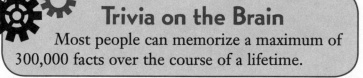

Trivia on the Brain
Most people can memorize a maximum of 300,000 facts over the course of a lifetime.

Answers on page 183.

T Is for Trail

Find 22 hidden objects in the scene below.

TABLE	TEPEE	TRACKS (ANIMAL)
TABLECLOTH	TENTS	TRAIN
TACKLE BOX	TIRE	TREES
TAIL	TOAD	TRIPOD
TEACUP	TOASTER	T-SHIRTS
TEAPOT	TODDLER	TURTLE
TELESCOPE	TOGA	
TENNIS RACQUET	TOP HAT	

Answer on page 183.

Word Ladder

Can you change just one letter on each line to transform the top word to the bottom word? Don't change the order of the letters, and make sure you have a common English word at each step.

WALK

_____ have a conversation

_____ a type of story

_____ available to buy

_____ not any different

_____ a few

HOME

Paper Fold

What word is written on this folded paper?

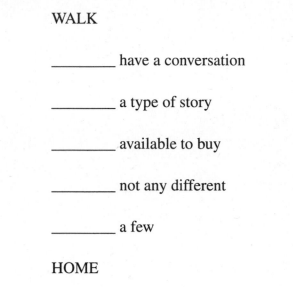

Answers on page 183.

Bricks and Rectangles

Which shape does not belong in this sequence?

Trivia on the Brain

Scientists have identified the specific area of the brain that causes laughter.

Answer on page 183.

Theme Park

This "ride" has a theme, but we can't tell you what it is. Place all the words in the boxes below—when you do, read the word created in the outlined boxes, from top to bottom, to reveal what the theme is.

VOLLEY BALL   BASKETBALL

BASEBALL   P.E.

SOCCER   FOOTBALL

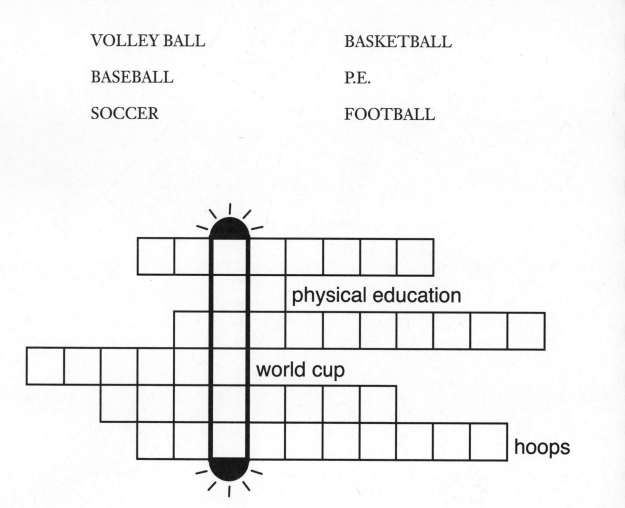

physical education

world cup

hoops

Answer on page 183.

Paper Fold

What musical instrument is written on this folded paper?

Chain Words

Place 3 letters in the middle squares that will complete one word and start another. For example, TAR would complete GUI - TAR - GET.

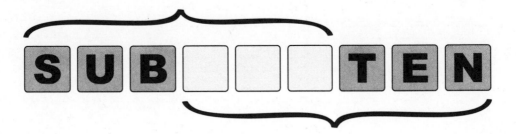

Answers on page 183.

Decoder

An old notebook was recently dug up in a baseball field. Use the code below to decipher the 2 riddles and their answers that are written in the book.

W[H][E]RE DO WE [F]IN[D] [P]I[R][A]TE[S] THAT
[D]ON'T [S]A[I]L [S][H]I[P]S, CA[R]R[Y] S[W][O][R][D]S,
OR [B]U[R][Y] [T][R]EA[S][U]RE?

ANSWER: [P]I[T][T]S[B]U[R][G]H, [P]A

* * *

[W]HER[E] D[O] WE F[I][N]D [D]I[A][M][O][N]DA[C][K]S
THAT ARE [R][E]D AND [B][L]A[C]CK, LI[V][E] IN THE
[D]E[S]ERT, BUT DON'T [H]AVE ANY [R][A]T[T][L]ES?

ANSWER: A[R]I[Z][O][N]A

A = (club)   B = (apple)   C = (fleur-de-lis)   D = (paintbrush)   E = (sun)

F = (bird)   G = (glasses)   H = (light bulb)   I = (safety pin)   J = (key)

K = (scissors)   L = (lock)   M = (TV)   N = (keys)   O = (telephone)

P = (hammer)   Q = (fan/asterisk)   R = (sock)   S = (clothespin)   T = (bone)

U = (alarm clock)   V = (hanger)   W = (watch)   X = (bathtub)   Y = (spoon)

Z = (arrow)

Answers on page 183.

kittens

Can you help each kitten find its ball of yarn?

Answers on page 183.

Riddle Scramble

Use the scrambled words to solve each of the clues below. Once you've done that, unscramble the letters found in the boxes to solve this riddle: I can live on land and water—what am I?

1. I use this part of my body as a shield.

2. Instead of these, I have ridges in my mouth for chewing food.

3. My legs are _____ in length.

4. I am cold-blooded and part of this family.

5. I lay my eggs in this.

6. Although I'm slow, I'm known to race against this.

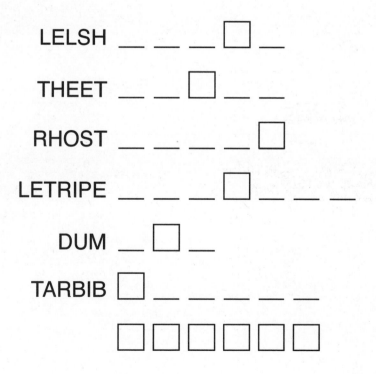

LELSH __ __ __ ☐ __

THEET __ __ ☐ __ __

RHOST __ __ __ __ ☐

LETRIPE __ __ __ ☐ __ __ __

DUM __ ☐ __

TARBIB ☐ __ __ __ __ __

☐ ☐ ☐ ☐ ☐ ☐

Answers on page 183.

Home Sweet Home

Can you find the 2 identical houses?

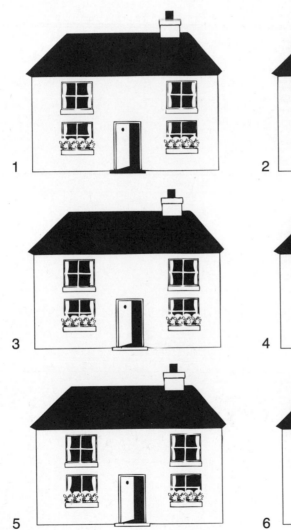

Answer on page 183.

Word Math

This puzzle works exactly like a regular math problem, but instead of using numbers in the equation you use letters. First, fill in the blanks with the proper name for each picture. Then solve the equation.

$+$ $-$ $=$ _ _ _ _ _ _ _

_ _ _ _ _ _ _ _ _ _ _ _ _ _ _

Flippy Numbers

Below is an incorrect equation. Can you swap 2 of the number cards to get a correct equation?

$$15 \times 2 = 60$$

Answers on pages 183–184.

Highland Fling

Can you find the 2 identical bagpipers?

Answer on page 184.

Food Anagrams

Unscramble the capital letters to discover the names of 5 types of food. Read some of the ingredients for extra help!

1. MR BEAR HUG

Lettuce

Tomato

Onions

— — — — — — — — —

2. PAIL PEEP

Apples

Flour

Sugar

Cinnamon

— — — — — — — —

3. SIGHT TAPE

Noodles

Tomato sauce

Meatballs

— — — — — — — — — —

4. MICE RACE

Cones

Select toppings (sprinkles, chocolate chips, syrup)

— — — — — — — —

5. CHECKUP IS ON

Carrots

Celery

Noodles

Broth

— — — — — — — —
— — — —

Answers on page 184.

Picture This

Copy the picture in each numbered square into the same numbered square in the grid to reveal this prowler.

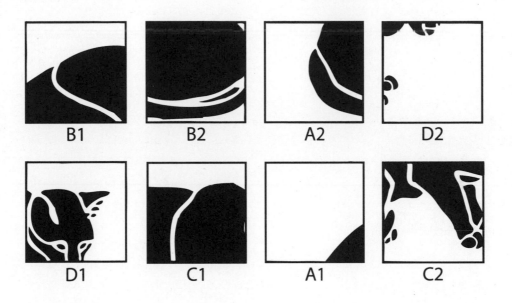

B1   B2   A2   D2

D1   C1   A1   C2

	A	B	C	D
1				
2				

Answer on page 184.

Mish—Mash

ACROSS

1. School group: abbr.
4. Pound: abbr.
6. Weather that's a cause of decreased visibility
9. What you do during lunch period
10. "Friend or _____?"
11. Confederate general Robert E. _____
12. Report card mark
14. Gain knowledge in class
16. Sink _____ swim
17. Los Angeles: abbr.
18. _____ card (record of grades)
22. Go bad
25. Hair coloring
26. Orange Thanksgiving food
28. "_____ you see that?"
30. DEAD _____ (road sign)
32. Loose-leaf holder
34. Elevator direction
36. Word of denial
37. Loose-leaf _____
40. Fire _____ (safety procedure)
44. Class involving painting, drawing, etc.
45. "For what _____ worth…"
47. Cow's call
48. "Absolutely!"
49. Fifteen, in Roman numerals
50. Wise bird

DOWN

1. _____ leg (pirate's artificial limb)
2. Paving material
3. "Now _____ theater near you!"
4. "_____ and behold!"
5. It rings at the end of class
6. Florida: abbr.
7. "_____ the ramparts we watched…"
8. General: abbr.
10. Car-carrying boat
13. Cartoon dog Scooby-_____
15. Organ of hearing
18. Road: abbr.
19. Part of a needle or potato
20. Writing need
21. Indent key, on a PC
23. Like the numbers 1, 3, 5, 7, etc.
24. _____ the knot (get married)
27. Pays attention to
29. Doctor: abbr.
31. Expected to arrive
33. Neither here _____ there
35. Grand _____ (auto race)
37. _____-per-view TV
38. YOU _____ HERE (words on a mall map)
39. Points: abbr.
41. "In my opinion," on the Net
42. Like poor grades

43. "Very funny!" in a chat room

46. "As seen on _____"

Trivia on the Brain
Our brains continue to generate new neurons throughout nearly all our lives—even into our seventies!

Answers on page 184.

Jungle Explorers

While these campers are exploring nature, explore these 2 pictures and see if you can find the 8 differences.

Answers on page 184.

Class Schedule

It's the beginning of the school year and Tom is starting junior high. Yesterday, he received his class schedule and he learned that there are 6 periods in a school day! Determine which period each class takes place.

1. Tom has algebra right after French class.

2. His last class is marching band.

3. He has U.S. history later in the day than his gym class.

4. During second period, Tom studies biology.

5. He doesn't have French in the third period.

	1	2	3	4	5	6
Algebra						
Biology						
French						
Gym						
Marching Band						
U.S. History						

Answer on page 184.

The Ocean

Every word listed is contained within the group of letters below. Words can be found in a straight line diagonally, horizontally, or vertically. They may be read either forward or backward.

```
S O T E S E A H O R S E H E
T E C E E N T P Y H E K L I
I R D T E B O M S L C A E R
N E O A O A A I T N H N R E
G L L N I P F R E W B S A B
R C P A S L U H R A E A L M
A A H M E T F S F A A E L U
Y N I G A N A Q H E C S O C
V R N E C R O U T A H U D U
O A S E D D N I H C R U D C
H B B I Y A P D L E B K N A
C O N C H N I L R A M B A E
N E L E C T R I C E E L S S
A N E M O N E G N O P S L E
```

ANCHOVY	DOLPHIN	SARDINE	SHRIMP
ANEMONE	ELECTRIC EEL	SEA CUCUMBER	SPONGE
ANGELFISH	MANATEE	SEAHORSE	SQUID
BARNACLE	MARLIN	SEA LION	STINGRAY
BARRACUDA	OCTOPUS	SEA SNAKE	URCHIN
BEACH	OYSTER	SEA TURTLE	WHALE
CONCH	SAND DOLLAR	SHARK	

Answers on page 184.

Mutations

Look at the 2 words on each line. Someone has not only scrambled the words from the left side to the right, but a letter has been removed as well! Figure out what that letter is and write it in the blank. When you're done, read the letters going down to answer this riddle: What game do parrots play?

POLISH ___ SPOIL

ONION ___ NOON

DENIM ___ MINE

EIGHTH ___ THIGH

LABEL ___ BELL

MELON ___ MOLE

ORCHID ___ CHOIR

PIE CRUST ___ PICTURE

SPRING ___ GRINS

ORANGE ___ GROANS

TASTE ___ TEST

KNIFE ___ FINE

Answer on page 184.

Cowboy

Which 2 cowboys are identical?

Answer on page 184.

Number Code: Sounds Like Food

First, solve each of the arithmetic problems. Then, find the corresponding letter in the number code at right. Write the letter for that number on the second dash. Reading down the column of letters will reveal the hidden words.

1. 5 × 2 = __ __

   2 × 6 = __ __

   5 × 5 = __ __

   9 × 2 = __ __

2. 3 × 5 = __ __

   4 × 6 = __ __

   2 × 12 = __ __

   4 × 4 = __ __

3. 3 × 7 = __ __

   2 × 8 = __ __

   4 × 3 = __ __

   13 × 2 = __ __

   3 × 8 = __ __

4. 2 × 11 = __ __

   3 × 6 = __ __

   6 × 4 = __ __

   10 × 2 = __ __

5. 7 × 3 = __ __

   3 × 3 = __ __

   2 × 7 = __ __

   4 × 5 = __ __

   6 × 2 = __ __

   4 × 2 = __ __

CODE

1. F	14. N
2. L	15. M
3. Z	16. T
4. C	17. G
5. J	18. R
6. H	19. V
7. O	20. D
8. Y	21. S
9. U	22. B
10. P	23. Q
11. W	24. E
12. A	25. I
13. X	26. K

Answers on page 184.

FEEL THE MENTAL BURN

Jungle

It looks like someone's been monkeying around with these images; can you spot all 8 differences?

Trivia on the Brain

Did you know that 95 percent of your brain is taken up by the communication network that runs between the remaining 5 percent of gray cells?

Answers on page 185.

Vex-a-Gon

Place the numbers 1 through 6 into the triangles of each hexagon. The numbers may be in any order, but they do not repeat within each hexagon shape (6-sided shape around each black dot).

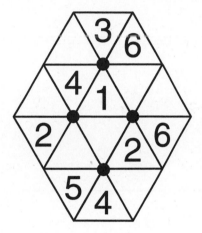

Word Ladder

Can you change just one letter on each line to transform the top word to the bottom word? Don't change the order of the letters, and make sure you have a common English word at each step.

CATS

_____ large rodents

_____ give a score to something

_____ what you do on a track

_____ white grain served as a side-dish

MICE

Answers on page 185.

Spiderweb

A butterfly is tangled in a spider's web; can you help her find the way out?

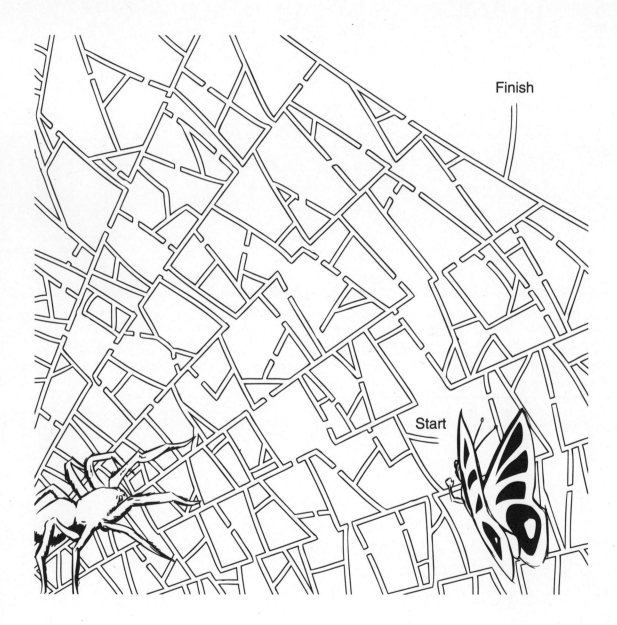

Finish

Start

Answer on page 185.

Matching Blots

Find the 2 blots that are identical to each other.

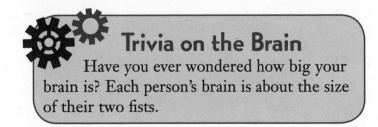

Trivia on the Brain

Have you ever wondered how big your brain is? Each person's brain is about the size of their two fists.

Answer on page 185.

Fun at the Circus

Every word listed is contained within the group of letters below. Words can be found in a straight line diagonally. They may be read either forward or backward.

BEARS

BIG TOP

CLOWNS

COTTON
   CANDY

ELEPHANTS

FIRE
   BREATHERS

FLYING
   TRAPEZE

HIGH WIRE

HORSES

HUMAN
   CANNONBALL

JUGGLING

LIONS

MAGIC SHOW

PEANUTS

PONIES

POPCORN

RINGMASTER

STRONGMAN

TENTS

TIGERS

TRAPEZE ACTS

```
H D F F K D S S U X Y S N E M R P J L P
J U C D M Y R T C H O P L Q C T U K N I
E T M C H E J D U D R E B G B G E T Y I
L P V A G K H Q Q N P I T Y G G C N F H
H W Y I N T W A K H A G N L C M E Z T G
Z O T Q C C H O A Y T E I G W T Q B S S
C S R X P V A N H R D N P Y M M F H R X
R P L S J U T N A I G N F M A A F F O Z
L R M N E S O P N I G L A G D I S N W G
G I Q I I S E K E O Y H I C R H Q T K N
U I O B R Z P J U I N C W E N R J M E O
Z P E N E C N J N N S B B I W O P O S R
S V H A S R B G A H D R A Q R H T Q J N
P X C S O I T M O C E D B L E E S T L D
I T B C P R G W J A D E S C L E F T O B
S D P T A N O T T X A X L E N C J S I C
G O G P O C G H F R J O V I I E S G Q V
P E E R V A E D S Z W Y S C J N T A A P
S Z T I D R P R F N S R D T K O O B I C
E S I C S J Y L S C V Y D J P Z L P Z K
```

Answers on page 185.

Paper Fold

What part of the body is written on this folded paper?

Flippy Numbers

Below is an incorrect equation. Can you swap 2 of the number cards to get a correct equation?

$$3 + 45 - 6 = 48$$

Answers on page 185.

Flower Growth

Which of these flowers has the longest stem?

Typewriter Error

Two fruits have been accidentally typed on top of each other. Can you decipher what they are?

Answers on page 185.

Mutations

Look at the 2 words on each line. Someone has not only scrambled the words from the left side to the right, but a letter has been removed as well! Figure out what that letter is and write it in the blank. When you're done, read the letters going down to answer this riddle: What do cowhands put on their pancakes?

MATCH ___ CHAT

LOAVES ___ SOLVE

PERSON ___ SNORE

CHAPEL ___ PEACH

OYSTER ___ STORY

LOWEST ___ TOWEL

RENTAL ___ LEARN

ADMIRES ___ DREAMS

RATHER ___ HEART

WINTER ___ TWINE

SAUCER ___ RACES

PRINCE ___ NICER

Answer on page 185.

Roman Senator

Which senator is the mirror image of the one in the box?

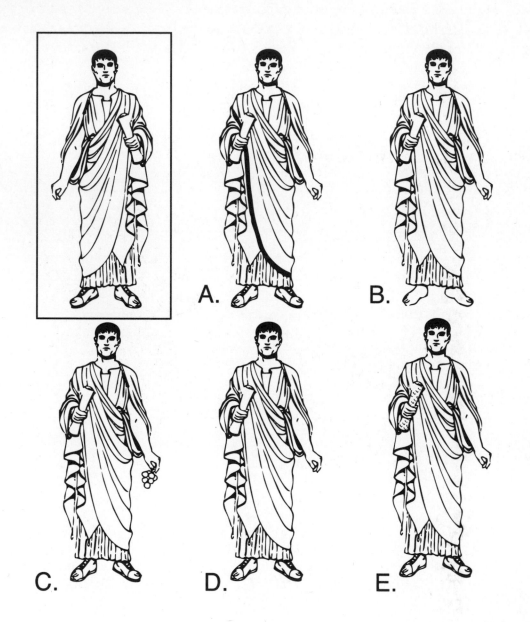

Answer on page 185.

Find the Blocks

Find the shapes at the right in the grid as many times as listed. The shapes must be facing the same direction as the examples.

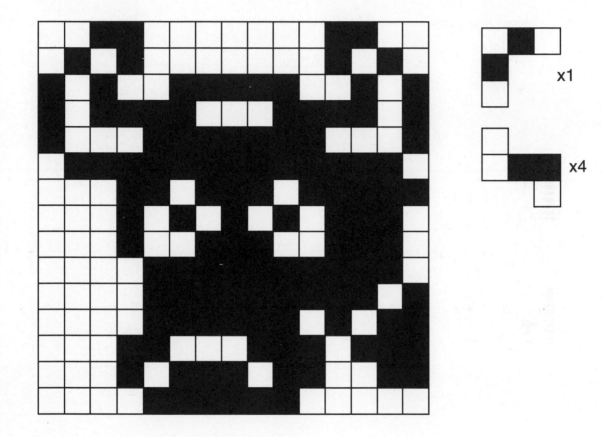

x1

x4

Answer on page 186.

113

Riddle in the Middle

Use the clues to complete the 5-letter answers, starting at the top and working your way down. When finished, read the letters in the squares with the thick boxes, from top to bottom, to reveal the answer to the riddle below.

What is full of holes but holds water?

1. Sticky glue

P [ ] [ ] E

2. Book material

P [ ] [ ] R

3. Approximately

A [ ] [ ] T

4. Underground worker

M [ ] [ ] R

5. Hot under the collar

A [ ] [ ] Y

6. Wool producers

S [ ] [ ] P

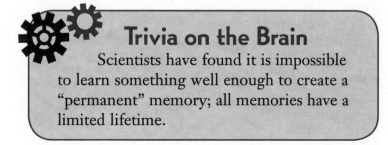

Trivia on the Brain

Scientists have found it is impossible to learn something well enough to create a "permanent" memory; all memories have a limited lifetime.

Answers on page 186.

1-2-3

Place the number 1, 2, or 3 in each empty circle. The challenge is to have only these 3 numbers in each connected row and column—no number should repeat. Any combination is allowed.

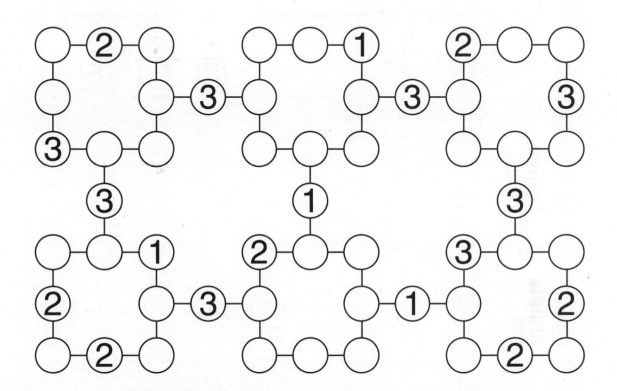

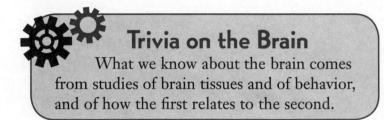

Trivia on the Brain

What we know about the brain comes from studies of brain tissues and of behavior, and of how the first relates to the second.

Answer on page 186.

Chain Words

Place 3 letters in the middle squares that will complete one word and start another. For example, TAR would complete GUI - TAR - GET.

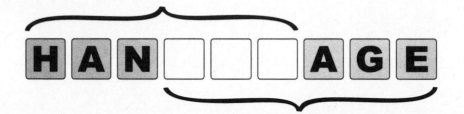

Word Math

This puzzle works exactly like a regular math problem, but instead of using numbers in the equation you use letters. First, fill in the blanks with the proper name for each picture. Then solve the equation.

Answers on page 186.

Theme Park

This "ride" has a theme, but we can't tell you what it is. Place all the words in the boxes below—when you do, read the word created in the outlined boxes, from top to bottom, to reveal what the theme is.

LOG CABIN   FOURSCORE

ILLINOIS   EMANCIPATION

HONEST   FIVE DOLLARS

CIVIL

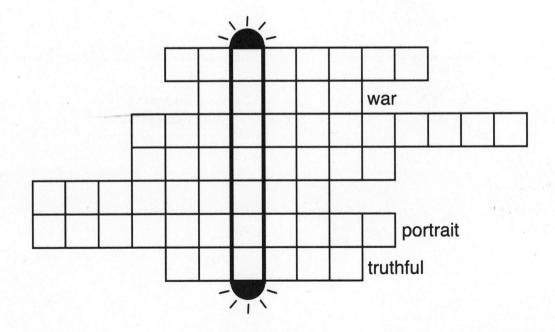

war

portrait

truthful

Answer on page 186.

Picture This

Copy the picture in each numbered square into the same numbered square in the grid to reveal something to help you rock on!

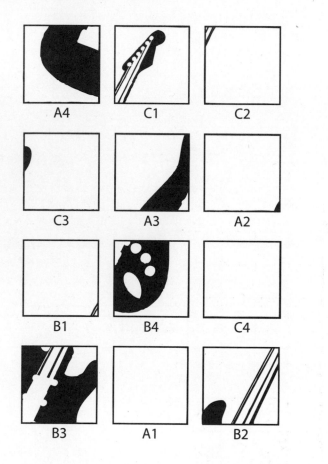

Answer on page 186.

Holiday Anagrams

Unscramble these letters to spell out the names of 5 holidays.

1. TEN LADIES NAVY

__ __ __ __ __ __ __ __ __ __' __   __ __ __ __

2. TIS CHARMS

__ __ __ __ __ __ __ __ __

3. A NEW HELLO

__ __ __ __ __ __ __ __ __

4. TV KING SANG HI

__ __ __ __ __ __ __ __ __ __ __ __ __

5. YARDSTICK SPAT

__ __.   __ __ __ __ __ __ __ __ __' __   __ __ __

Answers on page 186.

119

Desserts

Every word listed is contained within the group of letters below. Words can be found in a straight line diagonally, horizontally, or vertically. They may be read either forward or backward.

APPLE CRISP

BAKED ALASKA

BISCOTTI

BROWN BETTY

BROWNIE

CANDY BAR

CANNOLI

CARAMEL

CHERRY PIE

CHOCOLATE

CINNAMON ROLL

COOKIE

```
J E L L O O Y T T E B N W O R B B W P
I C E C R E A M C I T A L I A N I C E
I P O P S I C L E I T T O C S I B L D
N A K S A L A D E K A B H B O M P U C
G A E D J I M O U S S E R O V E E R H
X N M A R S H M A L L O W S A M I A O
P S I R C E L P P A W L H N F A P B C
I L J D F E U P E N L E U P E C Y Y O
L E E G D U F L I O R T I F K A R D L
O M L Y U U Z E R B B O R K T R R N A
N A L F K W P N E R N U C T O O E A T
N R Y F D X O T I Y I O S P Q O H C E
A A B A W M C T M T T D E I S N C W I
C C E T A X T U S A A S L L M D O E K
L V A N D L K A P N J L T I O A N W N
K E N Z E T L I I C K B O R R P R T I
U I S I H A O S W V A E R O E Y A I W
C O C H D C H J G L K K T G R A S N T
E P M H A T R U G O Y N E Z O R F E N
```

CUPCAKE

DANISH

ÉCLAIR

FROZEN YOGURT

FRUIT SALAD

FUDGE

ICE CREAM

ITALIAN ICE

JELL-O

JELLY BEANS

MACAROON

MARSHMALLOWS

MOUSSE

NAPOLEON

PEANUT BRITTLE

POPSICLE

PUDDING

SHERBET

S'MORE

TAFFY

TAPIOCA

TIRAMISU

TORTE

TWINKIE

Answers on page 186.

B Is for Beach

Find 23 hidden objects in the scene below.

BALL	BERET	BOW
BANANA	BIKINI	BOWL
BANJO	BINOCULARS	BOX
BASKET	BIRD	BREAD
BAT	BLANKET	BUBBLES
BEAR	BOAT	BULLDOG
BEAVER	BOOTS	BUTTERFLY
BELT	BOTTLE	

Answers on page 186.

Wired Shapes

Which shape does not belong in this sequence?

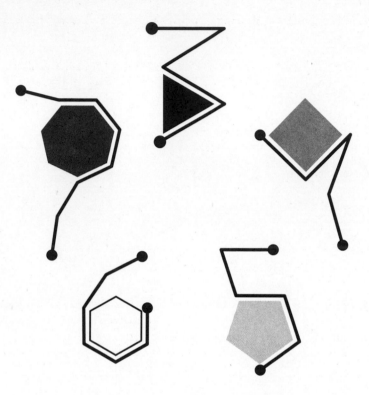

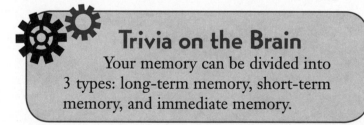

Trivia on the Brain
Your memory can be divided into 3 types: long-term memory, short-term memory, and immediate memory.

Answer on page 186.

Rhyme Time

Each clue leads to a 2-word answer that rhymes, such as BIG PIG or STABLE TABLE. The numbers in parentheses after the clue give the number of letters in each word. For example, "cookware taken from the oven (3, 3)" would be "hot pot."

1. What a watering can gives a garden to help it stay clean and green (6, 6): _____

2. Happy young man (4, 3): _____

3. Devours candy (4, 6): _____

4. Pile of hidden money (4, 5): _____

5. Impossible to screw up (4, 5): _____

6. What might come out of a pale-red pen (4, 3): _____

7. Alternate sibling (5, 7): _____

8. Rowdy activities (5, 5): _____

9. Nibble in half (4, 7): _____

10. Playground with no lights at night (4, 4): _____

11. Stone timepiece (4, 5): _____

12. Lecture on the sand (5, 6): _____

13. Skinnier person in the pool (7, 7): _____

14. Person looking for tennis shoes (7, 6): _____

15. A football or basketball star's watering devices (7, 8): _____

16. Dental detective (5, 6): _____

Answers on page 187.

Gerbils!

All these gerbils have huddled up for the night. How many can you count?

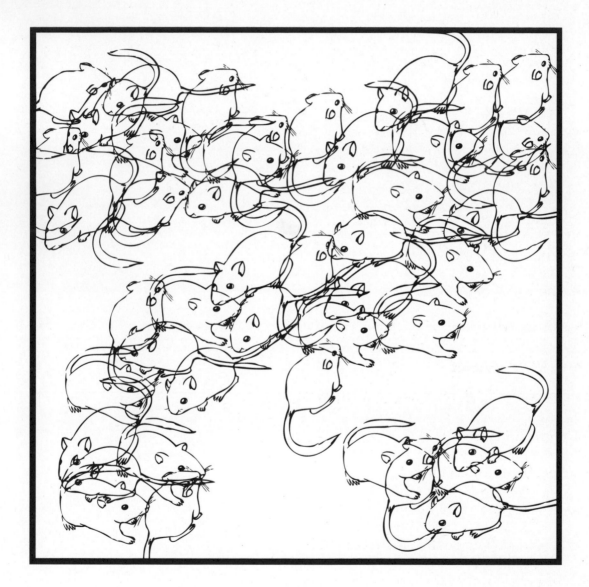

Answer on page 187.

Vex-a-Gon

Place the numbers 1 through 6 into the triangles of each hexagon. The numbers may be in any order, but they do not repeat within each hexagon shape (6-sided shape around each black dot).

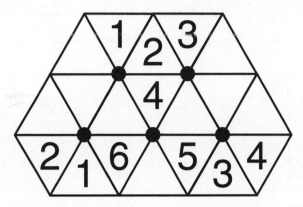

Word Ladder

Can you change just one letter on each line to transform the top word to the bottom word? Don't change the order of the letters, and make sure you have a common English word at each step.

LOSE

_____

_____

_____

FIND

Answers on page 187.

Picture This

Copy the picture in each numbered square into the same numbered square in the grid to reveal a playful pal.

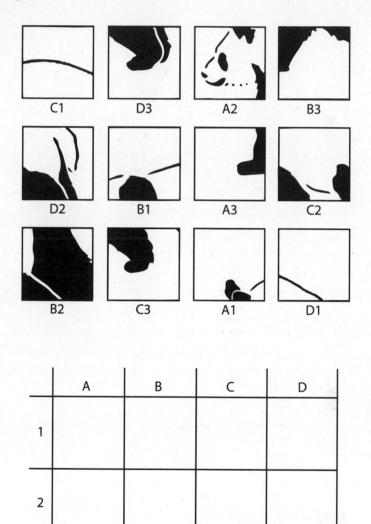

Answer on page 187.

Tangled Kites

Can you help each kid find their kite?

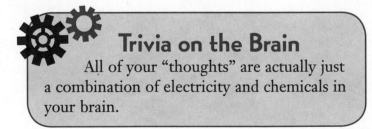

Trivia on the Brain

All of your "thoughts" are actually just a combination of electricity and chemicals in your brain.

Answers on page 187.

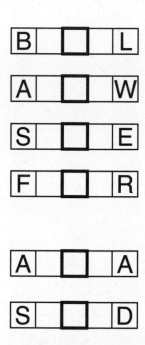

Riddle in the Middle

Use the clues to complete the 5-letter answers, starting at the top and working your way down. When finished, read the letters in the squares with the thick boxes, from top to bottom, to reveal the answer to the riddle below.

What does every living person do at the same time?

1. Breakfast item, with cream cheese   B [ ] L

2. Bow and _____   A [ ] W

3. Make a goal   S [ ] E

4. Less   F [ ] R

5. Cooking smell   A [ ] A

6. Not a gas or a liquid   S [ ] D

7. Beneath   U [ ] R

8. Traffic light color   G [ ] N

9. Wed   M [ ] Y

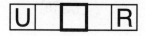
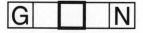
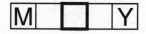

Answers on page 187.

Jammin'!

Can you spot the 8 rockin' differences between these 2 cool band scenes?

Answers on page 187.

Number Code: Presidents

First, solve each of the arithmetic problems. Then, find the corresponding letter in the number code at right. Write the letter for that number on the second dash. Reading down the column of letters will reveal the hidden words.

1. $14 + 4 - 13 =$ ___ ___

   $2 + 12 - 8 =$ ___ ___

   $20 + 2 - 9 =$ ___ ___

   $20 + 1 - 19 =$ ___ ___

   $12 + 9 - 16 =$ ___ ___

2. $8 + 6 - 12 =$ ___ ___

   $5 + 5 - 6 =$ ___ ___

   $13 + 18 - 6 =$ ___ ___

   $17 + 9 - 6 =$ ___ ___

   $31 + 4 - 10 =$ ___ ___

3. $13 + 2 - 14 =$ ___ ___

   $21 + 8 - 4 =$ ___ ___

   $6 + 20 - 7 =$ ___ ___

   $13 + 8 - 9 =$ ___ ___

   $4 + 21 - 7 =$ ___ ___

   $30 + 2 - 13 =$ ___ ___

4. $13 + 11 - 5 =$ ___ ___

   $21 + 13 - 16 =$ ___ ___

   $17 + 14 - 6 =$ ___ ___

   $13 + 18 - 24 =$ ___ ___

   $16 + 17 - 8 =$ ___ ___

   $12 + 9 - 16 =$ ___ ___

5. $5 + 15 - 8 =$ ___ ___

   $5 + 17 - 3 =$ ___ ___

   $12 + 12 - 3 =$ ___ ___

   $3 + 18 - 1 =$ ___ ___

   $18 + 8 - 1 =$ ___ ___

   $7 + 7 - 9 =$ ___ ___

CODE

1. C	14. Y
2. O	15. V
3. P	16. Z
4. B	17. H
5. N	18. E
6. I	19. R
7. G	20. M
8. D	21. U
9. F	22. W
10. S	23. Q
11. J	24. L
12. T	25. A
13. X	26. K

Answers on page 187.

Farmer Maze

Can you help the farmer bring this lost cow back to the farm?

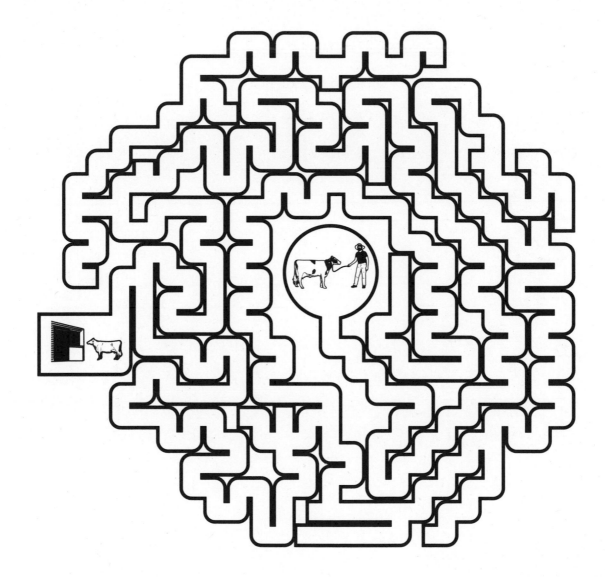

Answer on page 188.

Fit It

Figure out the names for each of the images below, then fit those names into the crossword grid.

ACROSS

DOWN

Answer on page 188.

Toy Store

There are 10 differences between these toy box scenes. Can you find them all?

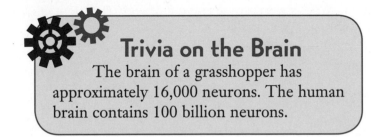

Trivia on the Brain

The brain of a grasshopper has approximately 16,000 neurons. The human brain contains 100 billion neurons.

Answers on page 188.

America

ACROSS

1. Limb used for walking
4. Tough _____ nails
6. Face the pitcher
9. Sailor's "yes"
10. _____ and reel
12. _____ de Janeiro, Brazil
13. Bic product
14. Lowest possible roll, with a pair of dice
15. Ginger _____ (soft drink)
16. Skating surface
18. Go down a slope
20. Organ that pumps blood
22. "I'm _____ your tricks!"
25. "Give _____ a break!"
26. "Are we there _____?"
28. Doctor: abbr.
29. Picnic spoilers
32. Musical symbols
35. Munch on
37. Neither here _____ there
38. "Honest _____" (presidential nickname)
40. Organization: abbr.
42. Limb that contains the biceps and triceps
45. Place to park cars
46. "_____ go, girl!"
47. Take to court
48. Ooh and _____

49. "In God _____ trust" (coin motto)
50. Put a stop to

DOWN

1. Once around the track
2. Sight organ
3. Spirit in a magic lamp
4. Line carrying blood from the heart
5. Scatter seed
6. Organ that controls learning
7. Feel ill
8. Digit on the foot
11. _____ and don'ts
17. California: abbr.
19. Knockout: abbr.
20. Egg-laying chicken
21. Number of fingers or toes
23. Touchdowns: abbr.
24. One _____ the other
25. Pa's wife
27. Organ containing taste buds
30. Molars, bicuspids, incisors, etc.
31. South America: abbr.
33. From top _____ bottom
34. Wipe off the board
36. Item in Santa's sack
38. Chicken _____ king
39. _____ constrictor (snake)
41. Use oars
43. Compete in a race
44. Size between small and large: abbr.

Answers on page 188.

Hoops

Get the ball to the net to make the winning basket and be MVP of the game.

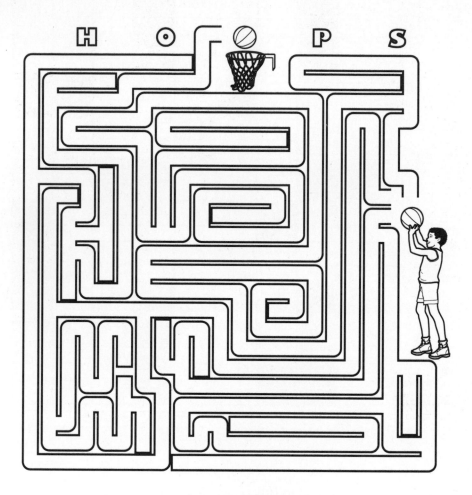

Answer on page 188.

Theme Park

This "ride" has a theme, but we can't tell you what it is. Place all the words in the boxes below—when you do, read the word created in the outlined boxes, from top to bottom, to reveal what the theme is.

SANTA   SHOPPING MALL

TREE   CAROLS

RUDOLPH   REINDEER

PRESENTS   SNOW

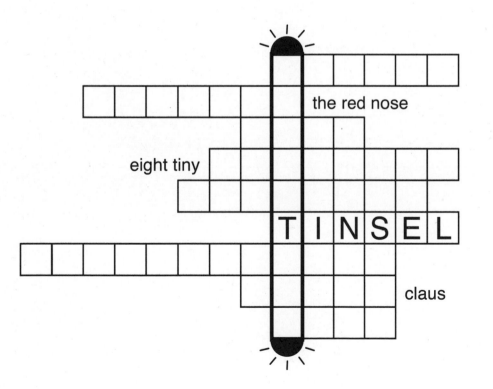

the red nose

eight tiny

T I N S E L

claus

Answer on page 188.

Apple Fun

Find 12 hidden objects in the scene below.

BANANA

BASEBALL BAT

BUTTON

CARROT

CUP

GOLF CLUB

LADLE

PENNANT

RING

RULER

SOCK

WORM

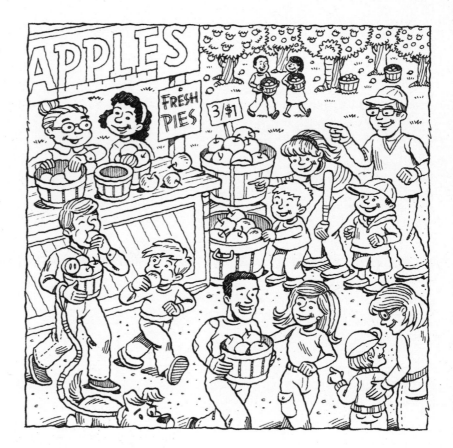

Answers on page 188.

Random Anagrams

Fill in the blanks in each sentence below with words that are anagrams (rearrangements of the same letters) of one another. The first one is done for you.

1. Jill <u>ATE</u> cookies with her <u>TEA</u>.

2. Robbie's _____ of soup was very hot, so he was careful to _____ on every spoonful.

3. In order to be the best magician around, Matthew started his _____ waving practice at the crack of _____.

4. Josie's _____ ate a _____ sandwich everyday for lunch and always smelled like fish!

5. The barnyard _____ flew _____ to avoid hitting the branch.

Answers on page 188.

Round 'em Up!

This cowboy has his work cut out for him! How many cows does he have to round up?

Answer on page 188.

Paper Fold

What word is written on this folded paper?

Flower Growth

Which of these flowers has the longest stem?

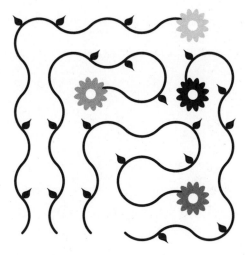

Answers on page 188.

A Day at the Beach

Answer the clues with words that will fit on the dotted lines. Then, find those answers in the grid. Words can be found in a straight line diagonally, horizontally, or vertically. They may be read either forward or backward.

1. What do you wear when you go swimming?

— — — — — —   — — — —

2. What's the name for the beachside pedestrian path?

— — — — — — — — —

3. What animal makes its home in empty seashells?

— — — — — — —   — — — —

4. What gooey animal can often wash up on the beach and cause quite a sting if you touch it?

— — — — — — — — — —

5. What kind of toy can you fly on the end of a string on a windy day at the beach?

— — — —

6. What do you use to protect your skin from the sun?

— — — — — — —

```
B O A R D W A L K I V P P L Z
E R W F E A A A E C Q S Y L U
L L U G A E S E D E E W A E S
X E M B A R C T I M R E H H J
A R Y E K L O I M C D U T S T
S J E E L W R K F N Y A H I R
E U S D E T L O T I O N U F A
A U N L R Q S A G B B S O Y L
S U K G B A A A L W G A W L L
H X M C L H O I C N T M A L E
E T Z D O A A B I D A S V E R
L O G O Y S S H F Y N V E J B
L X R B W C T S A R H A S Z M
Z U Q H W A J D E B U K S C U
R L K U B V H I S S S S A B S
```

7. What kind of watercraft uses the wind to move it across the water?

_ _ _ _ _ _ _

8. What can you build on the beach using only sand, a shovel, and a small bucket?

_ _ _ _ _ _ _ _ _ _

9. What's the name of the white-and-gray bird you commonly see at the beach?

_ _ _ _ _ _ _

10. What is the name for the exoskeleton of a marine mollusk? Hint: You see them on the beach all the time, and some people collect them!

_ _ _ _ _ _ _ _

11. What type of green-and-brown algae commonly washes up on the shore?

_ _ _ _ _ _ _

12. What do you wear to protect your eyes from the sun?

_ _ _ _ _ _ _ _ _

13. What do you use to "hang ten" on the ocean?

_ _ _ _ _ _ _ _

14. What do you use to dry yourself off after a swim?

_ _ _ _ _

15. What do you use at the beach to provide a nice shady spot to lie down in?

_ _ _ _ _ _ _

16. What do surfers need most to have a successful day on the ocean?

_ _ _ _ _

Answers on page 189.

Rhyme Time

Each clue leads to a 2-word answer that rhymes, such as BIG PIG or STABLE TABLE. The numbers in parentheses after the clue give the number of letters in each word. For example, "cookware taken from the oven (3, 3)" would be "hot pot."

1. Fight between cows (6, 6): _____

2. Bargain on rod's partner (4, 4): _____

3. Night crawler's cooties (5, 5): _____

4. Every individual fuzzy fruit (4, 5): _____

5. Person with the softer voice (6, 7): _____

6. Cow's male counterpart, after he's done eating (4, 4): _____

7. The best in any cabin at one particular thing (4, 5): _____

8. Drawing of spaghetti (6, 6): _____

9. Weird switch (7, 6): _____

10. Test for male sheep (3, 4): _____

11. Smarter author (8, 6): _____

12. Despises delays (5, 5): _____

13. Glum outlook (4, 4): _____

14. Show Francis gratitude (5, 5): _____

15. Woman shielded from the sun (5, 4): _____

16. Nicer memory aid (6, 8): _____

Answers on page 189.

Rapunzel

Help the prince reach Rapunzel by finding a way up the wall.

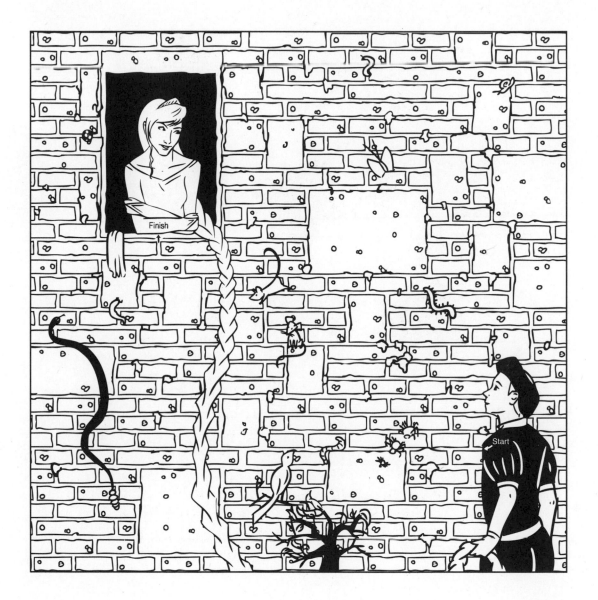

Answer on page 189.

Matching Blots

Find the 2 blots that are identical to each other.

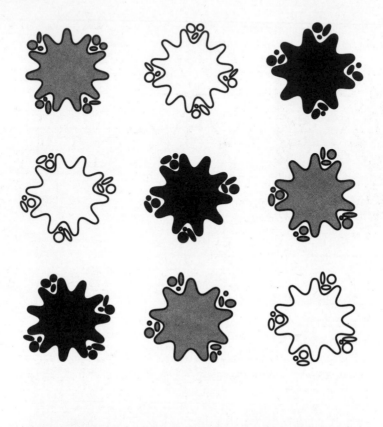

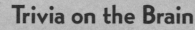 **Trivia on the Brain**

Are you sluggish in the morning? Start your day right by rehydrating your body. You've just spent a third of your day without drinking anything, and your brain needs water to function.

Answer on page 189.

Vex-a-Gon

Place the numbers 1 through 6 into the triangles of each hexagon. The numbers may be in any order, but they do not repeat within each hexagon shape (6-sided shape around each black dot).

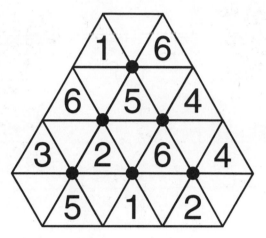

Typewriter Error

Two vehicles have been accidentally typed on top of each other. Can you decipher what they are?

Answers on page 189.

Picture This

Copy the picture in each numbered square into the same numbered square in the grid, matey!

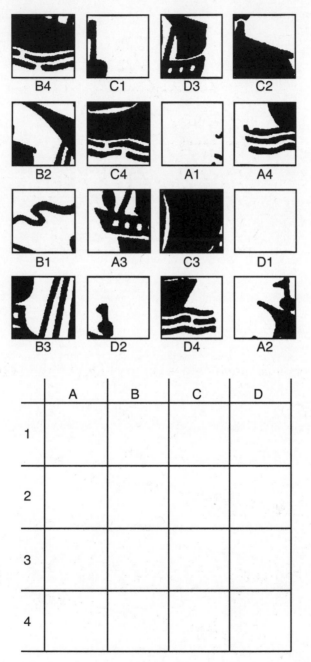

Answer on page 189.

Mutations

Look at the 2 words on each line. Someone has not only scrambled the words from the left side to the right, but a letter has been removed as well! Figure out what that letter is and write it in the blank. When you're done, read the letters going down to answer this riddle: What do you call a cardboard belt?

DARING ___ GRIND

WHINES ___ SHINE

SAFARI ___ FAIRS

ITCHES ___ CHEST

SELDOM ___ MODEL

SISTER ___ RISES

COPIES ___ SPICE

DIFFER ___ FRIED

PARCEL ___ CLEAR

RAISED ___ DRIES

SPROUT ___ TOURS

BEAVER ___ BRAVE

SPIDER ___ SPIED

Answers on page 189.

1-2-3

Place the number 1, 2, or 3 in each empty circle. The challenge is to have only these 3 numbers in each connected row and column—no number should repeat. Any combination is allowed.

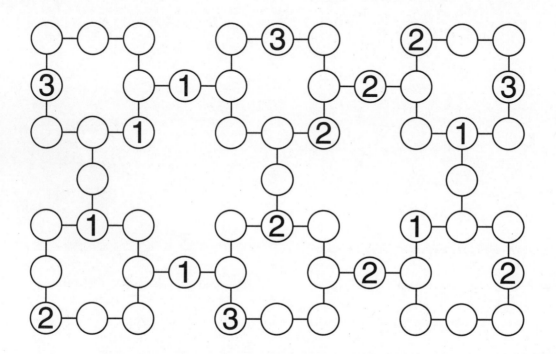

Trivia on the Brain

Of all the creatures on the earth, humans have the most complex brain.

Answer on page 189.

Paper Fold

What word is written on this folded paper?

Flippy Numbers

Below is an incorrect equation. Can you swap 2 of the number cards to get a correct equation?

$$2 \times 36 = 12$$

Answers on page 189.

Vex-a-Gon

Place the numbers 1 through 6 into the triangles of each hexagon. The numbers may be in any order, but they do not repeat within each hexagon shape (6-sided shape around each black dot).

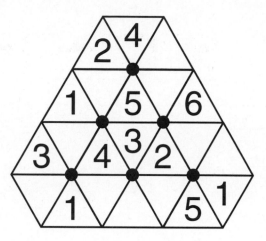

Word Ladder

Can you change just one letter on each line to transform the top word to the bottom word? Don't change the order of the letters, and make sure you have a common English word at each step.

SOME

———

———

———

MANY

Answers on pages 189–190.

Theme Park

This "ride" has a theme, but we can't tell you what it is. Place all the words in the boxes below—when you do, read the word created in the outlined boxes, from top to bottom, to reveal what the theme is.

LETTUCE   CABBAGE

TOMATO   SQUASH

BEANS   CUCUMBER

RADISH   BEETS

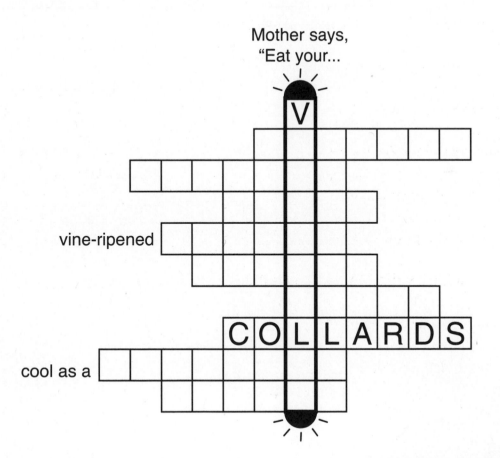

Mother says, "Eat your...

vine-ripened

COLLARDS

cool as a

Answers on page 190.

153

Rhyme Time

Each clue leads to a 2-word answer that rhymes, such as BIG PIG or STABLE TABLE. The numbers in parentheses after the clue give the number of letters in each word. For example, "cookware taken from the oven (3, 3)" would be "hot pot."

1. Skinny arm or leg (4, 4) _____

2. Plain shell-dweller (4, 4) _____

3. What usually holds a baseball together (3, 6) _____

4. Freshly uncovered hint (3, 4) _____

5. Contest of speed from planet to planet (5, 4) _____

6. Examination for visitors (5, 4) _____

7. A king's rocky seat (5, 6) _____

8. People with no money (5, 4) _____

9. Less-capable hospital helper (5, 5) _____

10. Lad's playthings (4, 4) _____

11. Stinky animal with a Mohawk and leather clothing (4, 5) _____

12. Confident walk, for a pup (4, 5) _____

13. Even-handed duo (4, 4) _____

Answers on page 190.

Flower Power

Which floral design is the mirror image of the one in the box?

Answer on page 190.

155

Riddle in the Middle

Use the clues to complete the 5-letter answers, starting from the top and working your way down. When complete, read the squares with the thick boxes, from top to bottom, to reveal the answer to the riddle below.

What can you hold without using your hands and save without needing a bank?

1. City leader   M ☐ R

2. Repeat word for word   Q ☐ E

3. Not old   Y ☐ G

4. Mistake   E ☐ R

5. Path around the Earth   O ☐ T

6. Stroke a guitar   S ☐ M

7. Sleeper's vision   D ☐ M

8. Long look   S ☐ E

9. Entire   T ☐ L

10. Remains of a fire   A ☐ S

Answers on page 190.

Matching Blots

Find the 2 blots that are identical to each other.

Trivia on the Brain

On average, the male brain is slightly larger than the female brain—but the differences in weight or size don't mean there are differences in mental ability.

Answer on page 190.

Number Code: States

First, solve each of the arithmetic problems. Then, find the corresponding letter in the number code at right. Write the letter for that number on the second dash. Reading down the column of letters will reveal the hidden words.

1. $12 \div 2 =$ ___ ___

$33 \div 3 =$ ___ ___

$20 \div 4 =$ ___ ___

$40 \div 20 =$ ___ ___

$24 \div 6 =$ ___ ___

2. $30 \div 5 =$ ___ ___

$56 \div 7 =$ ___ ___

$14 \div 7 =$ ___ ___

$65 \div 5 =$ ___ ___

$99 \div 9 =$ ___ ___

$8 \div 4 =$ ___ ___

$44 \div 4 =$ ___ ___

3. $24 \div 4 =$ ___ ___

$88 \div 8 =$ ___ ___

$36 \div 4 =$ ___ ___

$36 \div 2 =$ ___ ___

$75 \div 3 =$ ___ ___

$55 \div 5 =$ ___ ___

$26 \div 13 =$ ___ ___

$63 \div 3 =$ ___ ___

4. $48 \div 8 =$ ___ ___

$40 \div 8 =$ ___ ___

$35 \div 5 =$ ___ ___

$18 \div 6 =$ ___ ___

$50 \div 10 =$ ___ ___

$34 \div 2 =$ ___ ___

$77 \div 7 =$ ___ ___

$34 \div 17 =$ ___ ___

5. $60 \div 10 =$ ___ ___

$45 \div 9 =$ ___ ___

$36 \div 3 =$ ___ ___

$48 \div 4 =$ ___ ___

$72 \div 9 =$ ___ ___

$30 \div 2 =$ ___ ___

$72 \div 8 =$ ___ ___

$60 \div 12 =$ ___ ___

CODE

1. F	14. V
2. N	15. U
3. H	16. Z
4. E	17. G
5. I	18. Y
6. M	19. W
7. C	20. X
8. O	21. D
9. R	22. Q
10. P	23. J
11. A	24. K
12. S	25. L
13. T	26. B

Answers on page 190.

Flower Growth

Which of these flowers has the longest stem?

Vex-a-Gon

Place the numbers 1 through 6 into the triangles of each hexagon. The numbers may be in any order, but they do not repeat within each hexagon shape (6-sided shape around each black dot).

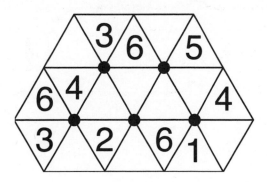

Answers on page 190.

Flippy Numbers

Below is an incorrect equation. Can you swap 2 of the number cards to get a correct equation?

$$81 \div 8 = 18$$

Chain Words

Place 3 letters in the middle squares that will complete one word and start another. For example, TAR would complete GUI - TAR - GET.

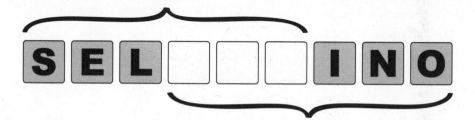

S E L [ ] [ ] [ ] I N O

Answers on page 190.

Halloween Costumes

Every word listed is contained within the group of letters below. Words can be found in a straight line diagonally. They may be read either forward or backward.

BARBIE

BATMAN

CAPTAIN AMERICA

CINDERELLA

DARTH VADER

DORA THE EXPLORER

GI JOE

HANNAH MONTANA

HARRY POTTER

THE INCREDIBLE
    HULK

INDIANA JONES

IRON MAN

KING KONG

THE LITTLE MERMAID

LUKE SKYWALKER

MICKEY MOUSE

MINNIE MOUSE

PINOCCHIO

POWER RANGER

SLEEPING BEAUTY

SPIDER-MAN

SUPERGIRL

SUPERMAN

TINKER BELL

WONDER WOMAN

```
S R R S M E N N X P W S A V B P P M D M
I X E U L Y H M A R I T G A F O C I Y T
U N J R V E E L E M I N R N W U A N T X
H W D V O S E D U N O B O E O M F T F H
Y A D I W L A P K M I W R C R K H D A Z
R H R N A V P E I E I R R E C E G N E R
A E M R H N R X S N A C M E I H N N A J
X S K T Y B A U E N G E K N D A I C I W
M N R L E P P J G E L B C E H N I O I K
U A A L A E O E O T H R E M Y R O E R N
D A L M R W R T T N E T O A E M S W A R
R H L G R Y Y I T D E N A M U U O M P P
O Q I L G E L K I E T S A R O T R U Z N
J R X I E E P B S A R N I M O E Y Q S H
L D J A H R L U N E I S E R D D W P N E
H O C T Q E E A S A K I Q I O U K A J A
E E J S H U D D T Q N U P P T N M K K L
W U T U L S S P N N E S L E K T M X Y G
K W L T T W A O I I S B T Y A Q M A X X
R K M L P C X M M V C U N B K W C X N C
```

Answers on page 191.

Theme Park

This "ride" has a theme, but we can't tell you what it is. Place all the words in the boxes below—when you do, read the word created in the outlined boxes, from top to bottom, to reveal what the theme is.

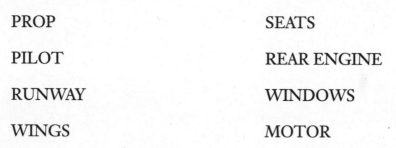

PROP	SEATS
PILOT	REAR ENGINE
RUNWAY	WINDOWS
WINGS	MOTOR

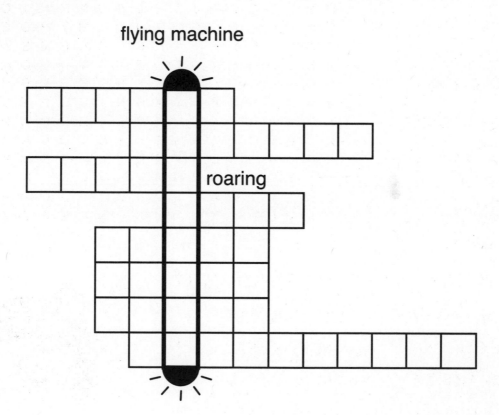

flying machine

roaring

Answers on page 191.

Insect Anagrams

Unscramble the letters to spell the names of 8 common insects. Then read all the boxed letters in order to find out the answer to this riddle: Why wouldn't they let the butterfly into the dance?

SO TO QUIM

▢ _ _ _ _ _ _ _

ANGRY FOLD

_ _ _ _ ▢ _ _ _ _

TRY ELF TUB

_ _ _ ▢ _ _ _ _ _

GRAPH SPORES

_ _ _ _ _ _ ▢ _ _ _ _ _

BALD GUY

_ _ _ _ ▢ _ _

A RILL CARPET

_ ▢ _ _ _ _ _ _ _ _

LET BEE

_ _ _ _ ▢ _

FRY HOLES

_ _ _ _ _ _ ▢ _

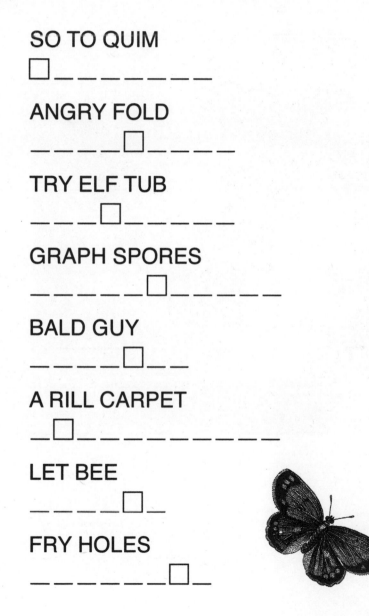

Answers on page 191.

Find the Blocks

Find the shapes at the right in the grid as many times as listed. The shapes must be facing the same direction as the examples.

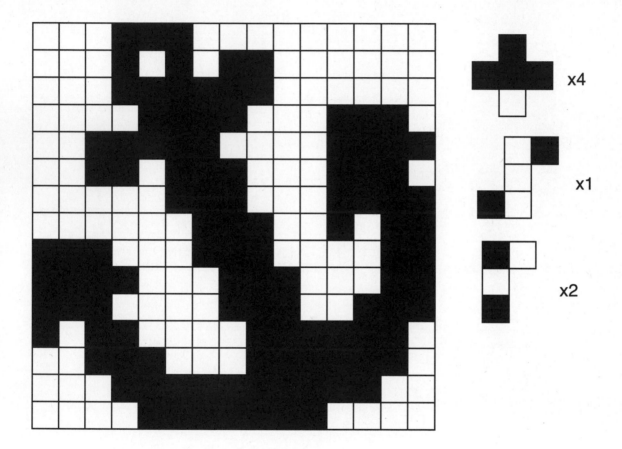

x4

x1

x2

Answer on page 191.

Fit It

Figure out the names for each of the images below, then fit those names into the crossword grid.

ACROSS

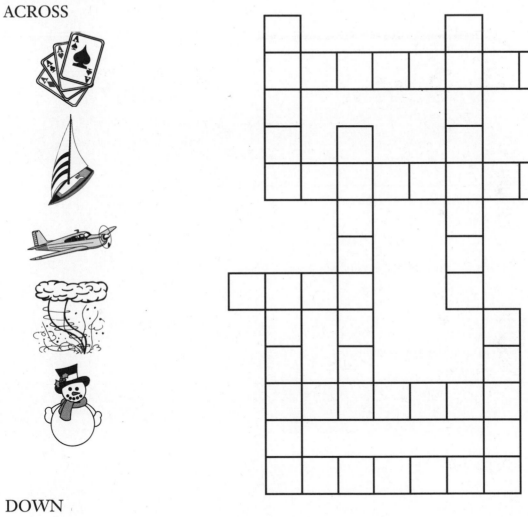

DOWN

Answer on page 191.

Chain Words

Place 3 letters in the middle squares that will complete one word and start another. For example, TAR would complete GUI - TAR - GET.

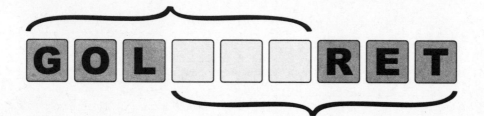

Word Math

This puzzle works exactly like a regular math problem, but instead of using numbers in the equation you use letters. First, fill in the blanks with the proper name for each picture. Then solve the equation.

Answers on page 191.

Fishing

Can you find your way through the tangled fishing line to reel in your catch?

Answer on page 191.

Math Class

ACROSS

1. Close friend
4. The total of
7. Find the total of
10. Our land: abbr.
11. "_____ Little Teapot"
12. Space between teeth
13. Times _____ (math memorization)
15. Flash _____ (math drill aids)
17. "Do _____ I say!"
18. "Yes," in Spain or Italy
19. Spaghetti, macaroni, etc.
22. Mathematical average
26. Alley _____ (basketball pass)
27. Tummy muscles, for short
29. Huge bird ridden by Sinbad
30. Number you shouldn't divide by
32. Having the same value
34. Number approximately equal to 3.14159
36. You and me
37. 3 × 3 × 3 = 3 _____
40. Remains of a campfire
44. The result of a number divided by itself
45. Corn portion
47. "_____ had it up to here!"
48. Coffee or flower holder
49. Fruity drink
50. Morning moisture

DOWN

1. Shot _____ (track & field event)
2. Strong _____ bull
3. Science classroom: abbr.
4. Mexican's nap
5. Sound of hesitation
6. Apple computers
7. Agriculture: abbr.
8. Mom's spouse
9. Double plays: abbr.
14. _____ Vegas, Nevada
16. "Ready, _____, fire!"
19. "The Raven" poet Edgar Allan _____
20. Fourth month: abbr.
21. "Honest _____" Lincoln
23. Period in history
24. "You've got mail" Internet co.
25. North Carolina: abbr.
26. Ounces: abbr.
28. Figure with 4 equal sides and 4 equal angles
31. Open, in poetry
33. "Star Trek" vessel, the _____ Enterprise
35. "What's the big _____?"
37. Policeman
38. Card game with Skip and Reverse cards
39. Put chips in a pot
41. Stayed out of sight

42. New Year's _____
43. Do some stitching
46. Pop-up _____ (PC nuisance)

Answers on page 191.

Birds

How many birds are in this picture?

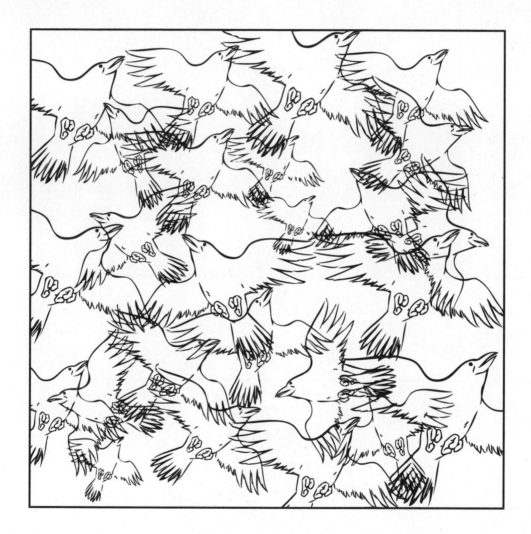

Answer on page 191.

USA Anagrams

Unscramble the letters to discover the names of 5 states in the United States. Once you've done this, match the states with their capitals.

1. IRON FACIAL

— — — — — — — — — — —

2. SATEX

— — — — —

3. AIR FOLD

— — — — — — —

4. WORN KEY

— — —   — — — —

5. WAIAIH

— — — — — —

Austin

Honolulu

Sacramento

Tallahassee

Albany

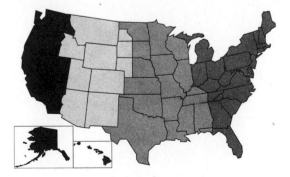

Answers on page 191.

Picture This

Copy the picture in each numbered square into the same numbered square in the grid, to reveal this trusty companion.

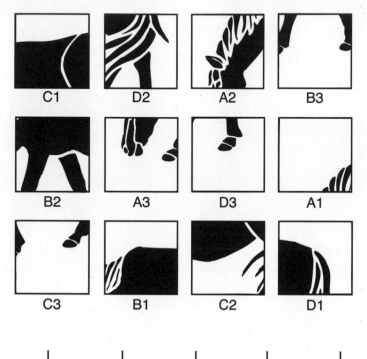

	A	B	C	D
1				
2				
3				

Answer on page 191.

Paper Fold

What word is written on this folded paper?

Word Math

This puzzle works exactly like a regular math problem, but instead of using numbers in the equation you use letters. First, fill in the blanks with the proper name for each picture. Then solve the equation.

Answers on page 192.

Fruits

Every word listed is contained within the group of letters below. Words can be found in a straight line diagonally, horizontally, or vertically. They may be read either forward or backward.

APPLE

AVOCADO

BANANA

BLUEBERRY

CATAWBA

CHERRY

COSTARD

CRANBERRY

CURRANT

DAMSON

DATE

DRUPE

DURIAN

FIG

GOOSEBERRY

GRAPE

JAPONICA

KIWI

KUMQUAT

LEMON

LIME

LOGANBERRY

LOQUAT

MANGO

MEDLAR

MULBERRY

NECTARINE

OLIVE

ORANGE

PAPAYA

PEACH

PEAR

PERSIMMON

POMELO

PRUNE

QUINCE

RAISIN

SLOE

TAMARIND

TANGELO

TANGERINE

VICTORINE

WHORTLEBERRY

```
J Y N P P N B M D R A T S O C
R T Q M Q B A N A N A G L I O
P A P A Y A G Y E N L E W Y H
R U L B D R C R B Q G I F R A
U Q O L N K R J A N K O M R P
N M Q U I N C E A P D A T E P
E U U E R C I T B P E A R B L
E K A B A Y H S N N O T T N E
A N T E M E R E I H A N P A N
B N I R A P K R R A A G I R I
W H O R T L E B E R R Y O C R
A E C Y O G D R R B Y J A L A
T G Z A N T A U S A E O G V T
A N K A E L C M R I L S O N C
C A T I D P A I B I M C O L E
Y R R E B L U M V D A M S O N
P O M E L O E E C D E N O E G
D H M D R U P E O L S Q K N L
```

Answers on page 192.

ANSWERS

Weather Terms (page 6)

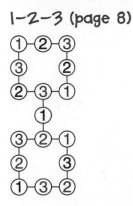

Rhyme Time (page 7)
1. fatter batter; 2. dinner winner; 3. wee sea;
4. neater eater; 5. must trust; 6. proud cloud

1-2-3 (page 8)

Honey Bear (page 9)

Road Trip! (page 10)

Matching Blots (page 11)

Mutations (page 12)
On a buzz!

Typewriter Error (page 12)
Bat, Pig

Decoder (page 13)
Out clubbing

Flower Growth (page 14)

Word Ladder (page 14)
Answers may vary.
WEE, bee, beg, BIG

Answers

Find the Blocks (page 15)

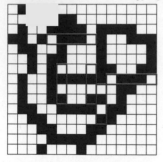

Treasure Chests (page 16)

There are 6 treasure chests.

Number Code: Any Questions? (page 17)

1. 5 + 10 = 15 W
   3 + 9 = 12 H
   4 + 4 = 8 O
2. 9 + 6 = 15 W
   7 + 5 = 12 H
   4 + 3 = 7 A
   6 + 3 = 9 T
3. 8 + 7 = 15 W
   11 + 1 = 12 H
   6 + 12 = 18 E
   3 + 2 = 5 N

4. 4 + 11 = 15 W
   2 + 10 = 12 H
   7 + 11 = 18 E
   2 + 4 = 6 R
   15 + 3 = 18 E
5. 12 + 3 = 15 W
   8 + 4 = 12 H
   9 + 7 = 16 Y

Picture This (page 18)

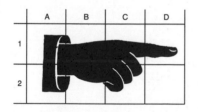

Riddle Scramble (page 19)

F U N

F L O A T

O C E A N

A I R

R A F T

Flippy Numbers (page 20)

1 + 2 + 3 = 5 + 7

1 + 5 + 3 = 2 + 7

Paper Fold (page 20)

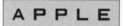

A P P L E

Find the Mice (page 21)

Theme Park (page 22)

```
      B
SURPRISE
 ICECREAM
 PARTY
     THEME
FRIENDS
    CAKE
    Y
```

Vex-a-Gon (page 23)

Paper Fold (page 23)

GOLF

Crazy Maze (page 24)

Polyshapes (page 25)

Each shape signifies a number and is made up of that number of shapes, except for 7, which is made up of only 6 shapes.

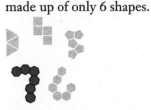

Marty the Moose (page 26)

9 friends are coming.

Word Ladder (page 27)

EASY, east, cast, cart, card, HARD

Chain Words (page 28)

BOTTOMATO

Word Math (page 28)

FAN − TABLE + ANT = CRADLE

Report Card (page 29)

English: A; math: A; social studies: B; science: B; Spanish: C. Since his English grade is better than his science grade (1), and his science grade is better than his Spanish grade (3), he must have gotten an A in English, a B in science, and a C in Spanish. He got an A in math (4). Since he didn't get an A in social studies (2), by elimination he got a B in social studies.

Number Anagram (page 30)

Burn; me; numb; men; rub; be

Paper Fold (page 30)

BELT

G Is for Ghost! (page 31)

Aye, Matey! (pages 32–33)

P	A	L		P	E	T		S	P	A
A	G	E		A	L	I		E	A	R
R	O	G	E	R		P	L	A	N	K
		S	R		S	O				
	B	I	S	O	N		S	M	E	E
P	A	D		T	O	M		A	T	M
G	R	O	G		T	U	R	N	S	
		E	P		T	O				
S	K	U	L	L		I	N	T	R	O
H	I	S		O	W	N		R	U	N
O	N	E		W	A	Y		A	M	S

Answers

Nice Trike (page 34)
B. In A, there are shadows under the wheels; C is missing front spokes.

Fit It (page 35)

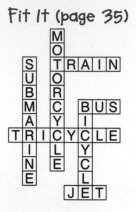

Bugs! (page 36)
Appears 5 times.

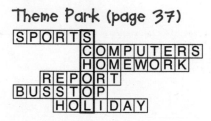

Theme Park (page 37)

Brave Knights (page 38)

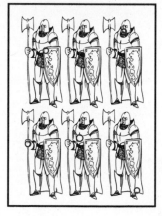

Home Sweet Home (page 39)

At the Ball (page 40)
Girls 2 and 4 are dressed the same.

1-2-3 (page 41)

Flower Growth (page 42)

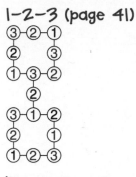

Chain Words (page 42)

RECENTITY

Rhyme Time (page 43)
1. older boulder; 2. bicker quicker; 3. Larry's cherries; 4. brown gown; 5. smelly jelly; 6. new shoe; 7. greater skater; 8. buy pie; 9. mail scale

School Days (page 44)

```
G N I L L E P S R B
T E A C H E R K 7 I
M Y O R B L I O L S
A U L G N E N C I T
T H S N R S C B W U
H Z Z I Q A I W R D
K S E D C E P A A E
L C H A I R A H R N
R E C E S S L R Y
C H W R I T I N G T
```

Mutations (page 45)

A cheetah!

Riddle in the Middle (page 46)

U P **S** E T

A R **M** O R

T R **A** I N

B E L **L** Y

C O **L** O R

Matching Blots (page 47)

Find the Blocks (page 48)

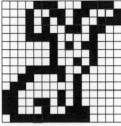

Vex-a-Gon (page 49)

Word Ladder (page 49)

BAIT, bail, boil, coil, cool, cook, HOOK

Crosspic (page 50)

```
8 E I G H T      A N
  Y          A   N   B
  E          I   T O E S
  S   T R E E S   N
      O           G
2 T W O   W A T C H
      T       R   A   S
    C H A I R   R   N O
      O       O   D   O
      S T R A W   S A W
```

Chain Words (page 51)

S A M P L E A S E

Flippy Numbers (page 51)

$3 \times 9 = 46$

↓

$4 \times 9 = 36$

Picture This (page 52)

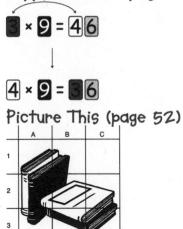

Decoder (page 53)

Knife; bread; needle; cheese; thread; apples; milk; mask
Items for surgery: Knife; needle; thread; mask

Riddle Scramble (page 54)

D I G

W A **G** S

N **O** S E

D O G

Answers

Fit It (page 55)

Circled Digits (page 56)

The circle around each number contains the same number of pieces, except for 7, which has 8 pieces.

Word Math (page 57)

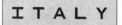

CART + BALLOON − BALL = <u>CARTOON</u>

Paper Fold (page 57)

I T A L Y

H Is for House (page 58)

Theme Park (page 59)

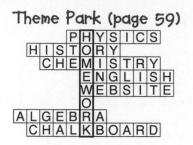

Peter the Polar Bear (page 60)

Bird Anagram (page 61)

Quail; seagull; eagle; crow; parakeet; ostrich; toucan; penguin

Riddle answer: He quacks up!

Number Code: J–Boys (page 62)

1. $15 + 1 - 12 = 4$ J
   $3 + 7 - 8 = 2$ O
   $7 + 1 - 5 = 3$ H
   $16 + 4 - 11 = 9$ N
2. $18 + 1 - 15 = 4$ J
   $2 + 13 - 8 = 7$ A
   $22 + 2 - 19 = 5$ R
   $4 + 7 - 10 = 1$ E
   $13 + 12 - 2 = 23$ D
3. $17 + 7 - 20 = 4$ J
   $11 + 8 - 18 = 1$ E
   $15 + 1 - 11 = 5$ R
   $9 + 3 - 11 = 1$ E
   $9 + 4 - 7 = 6$ M
   $12 + 9 - 10 = 11$ Y

4. $13 + 8 - 17 = 4$ J
   $10 + 1 - 9 = 2$ O
   $27 + 4 - 21 = 10$ S
   $5 + 6 - 8 = 3$ H
   $6 + 7 - 5 = 8$ U
   $18 + 5 - 16 = 7$ A
5. $5 + 5 - 6 = 4$ J
   $7 + 9 - 14 = 2$ O
   $24 + 5 - 20 = 9$ N
   $13 + 8 - 14 = 7$ A
   $17 + 5 - 10 = 12$ T
   $8 + 8 - 13 = 3$ H
   $6 + 2 - 1 = 7$ A
   $8 + 8 - 7 = 9$ N

On the Bus (page 63)

Emily, North Road, 2nd; Marcia, West Street, 1st; Patti, South Road, 4th; Sara, East Street, 3rd.

Patti is the fourth to be picked up (2). Since Marcia is picked up before the friend who lives on North Road who is picked up before Sara (6), Marcia must have been picked up first, the friend on North Road second, and Sara third. Therefore, Marcia lives on West Street (4). Sara isn't picked up on South Road (5), so by elimination, Sara is picked up on East Street, and Patti is picked up on South Road. Also by elimination, Emily is the second picked up.

Here Be Treasure! (page 64)

Game Time! (page 65)

Getting There (pages 66–67)

Waterspout (page 68)

Theme Park (page 69)

Rose Red (page 70)

A. In B, there is another flower instead of leaves; in C, the top branch is missing.

Crazy Maze (page 71)

Answers

1-2-3 (page 72)

Matching Blots (page 73)

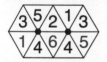

Vex-a-Gon (page 74)

3 5 2 1 3
1 4 6 4 5

Typewriter Error (page 74)
Jug, Pan

Ducks (page 75)

Fit It (page 76)

Flower Growth (page 77)

Word Ladder (page 77)
Answers may vary.
SICK, silk, sill, sell, WELL

Find the Blocks (page 78)

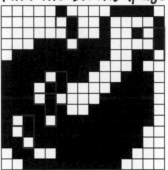

Numbers (page 79)

```
M U S D G H T H I R T Y
A C Y D E R D N U H W W
Z L D N A S U O H T E M
N E E T F I F I W L L W
I L F I T X L L S T V S
N G O E G T Q L O N E T
E E R H T H Y I T V J
M X T I T T M E R I I
O O Y I F C N N S E F E
B Q H I X P E L E V E N
C M F F F Y W J K O D B
O J T H I R T E E N I Z
```

Rhyme Time (page 80)
1. black shack; 2. gator hater; 3. crafts rafts;
4. split pit; 5. quick pick; 6. least east; 7. slight
fight; 8. great trait; 9. fox socks; 10. bug hug;
11. loose goose; 12. whole bowl

Clear as Day (page 81)
D. In A, his hat has a stripe; in B, he is holding a
fish; in C, the bucket is missing its handle.

Riddle in the Middle (page 82)

M I L E S
S T I L L
A L B U M
T H R E E
G R A P E
S T R I P
R O Y A L

T Is for Trail (page 83)

Word Ladder (page 84)

WALK, talk, tale, sale, same, some, HOME

Paper Fold (page 84)

S T O R Y

Bricks and Rectangles (page 85)

All the other "white" numbers contain darker pieces equal to their value.

Theme Park (page 86)

BASEBALL
PE
VOLLEYBALL
SOCCER
FOOTBALL
BASKETBALL

Paper Fold (page 87)

F L U T E

Chain Words (page 87)

S U B M I T T E N

Baseball Humor (page 88)

Where do we find pirates that don't sail ships, carry swords, or bury treasure? Pittsburgh, PA
Where do we find diamondbacks that are red and black, live in the desert, but don't have any rattles? Arizona

Kittens (page 89)

1. C; 2. A; 3. D; 4. B

Riddle Scramble (page 90)

S H E L L
T E E T H
S H O R T
R E P T I L E
M U D
R A B B I T
T U R T L E

Home Sweet Home (page 91)

3 and 6. In 1, a window is missing a curtain, and the threshold is black; in 2, the door is missing the peephole, and a window is missing panes; in 4, a window is missing panes, and the threshold is black; in 5, a window is missing panes, and another window is missing a curtain.

Word Math (page 92)

= S L I C E

SHIP POLICE HIPPO

Answers

Flippy Numbers (page 92)

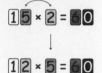

Highland Fling (page 93)

1 and 5. In 2, his spats have buttons, and his cap is missing the tassel; in 3, his sleeve is missing a stripe, and his socks are missing some plaid; in 4, his spats have buttons, and his sleeve is missing a stripe; in 6, his socks are missing some plaid and, his cap is missing the tassel.

Food Anagrams (page 94)

1. hamburger; 2. apple pie; 3. spaghetti; 4. ice cream; 5. chicken soup

Picture This (page 95)

Mish—Mash (pages 96—97)

Jungle Explorers (page 98)

Class Schedule (page 99)

Algebra, period 5; Biology, period 2; French, period 4; gym, period 1; marching band, period 6; U.S. history, period 3.

In period 2, Tom has biology class (4). Tom spent period 6 in the marching band class (2). Since he doesn't have French during the third period (5) but he has algebra right after his French class (1), he must have French during period 4 and algebra during period 5. Since he has U.S. history later in the day than gym (3), he has gym during period 1 and U.S. history during period 3.

The Ocean (page 100)

Mutations (page 101)

Hide and speak!

Cowboy (page 102)

A and D. B and C have different star designs on their vests and C has fewer decorations on the right side of his pants.

Number Code: Sounds Like Food (page 103)

1. $5 \times 2 = 10$ P
   $2 \times 6 = 12$ A
   $5 \times 5 = 25$ I
   $9 \times 2 = 18$ R
2. $3 \times 5 = 15$ M
   $4 \times 6 = 24$ E
   $2 \times 12 = 24$ E
   $4 \times 4 = 16$ T
3. $3 \times 7 = 21$ S
   $2 \times 8 = 16$ T
   $4 \times 3 = 12$ A
   $13 \times 2 = 26$ K
   $3 \times 8 = 24$ E
4. $2 \times 11 = 22$ B
   $3 \times 6 = 18$ R
   $6 \times 4 = 24$ E
   $10 \times 2 = 20$ D
5. $7 \times 3 = 21$ S
   $3 \times 3 = 9$ U
   $2 \times 7 = 14$ N
   $4 \times 5 = 20$ D
   $6 \times 2 = 12$ A
   $4 \times 2 = 8$ Y

Jungle (page 104)

Vex-a-Gon (page 105)

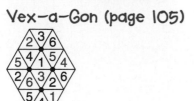

Word Ladder (page 105)
CATS, rats, rate, race, rice, MICE

Spiderweb (page 106)

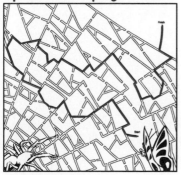

Matching Blots (page 107)

Fun at the Circus (page 108)

Paper Fold (page 109)

T O O T H

Flippy Numbers (page 109)

3 + 45 - 6 = 48

3 + 48 - 6 = 45

Flower Growth (page 110)

Typewriter Error (page 110)
Melon, Peach

Mutations (page 111)
Maple stirrup!

Roman Senator (page 112)
D. In A, he has a stripe on his toga; in B, he is barefoot; in C, he is holding a bunch of grapes; in E, there is writing on the scroll.

Answers

Find the Blocks (page 113)

Riddle in the Middle (page 114)

PA**ST**E

PA**PE**R

AB**OU**T

MI**NE**R

AN**GR**Y

SH**EE**P

1-2-3 (page 115)

Chain Words (page 116)

HANG**ARA**GE

Word Math (page 116)

ANT   EAGLE   TEA   = ANGLE

Theme Park (page 117)

ILLINOIS
CIVIL
EMANCIPATION
LOGCABIN
FOURSCORE
FIVEDOLLARS
HONEST

Picture This (page 118)

Holiday Anagrams (page 119)

1. Valentine's Day; 2. Christmas; 3. Halloween;
4. Thanksgiving; 5. St. Patrick's Day

Desserts (page 120)

B Is for Beach (page 121)

Wired Shapes (page 122)

All other number shapes contain line segments
equal to their value.

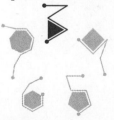

Rhyme Time (page 123)

1. flower shower; 2. glad lad; 3. eats sweets;
4. cash stash; 5. goof proof; 6. pink ink; 7. other
brother; 8. rough stuff; 9. chew through; 10. dark
park; 11. rock clock; 12. beach speech;
13. slimmer swimmer; 14. sneaker seeker;
15. player's sprayers; 16. tooth sleuth

Gerbils! (page 124)

There are 46 gerbils.

Vex-a-Gon (page 125)

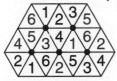

Word Ladder (page 125)

Answers may vary.
LOSE, lone, line, fine, FIND

Picture This (page 126)

Tangled Kites (page 127)

Riddle in the Middle (page 128)

BA**GE**L
AR**RO**W
SC**OR**E
FE**ME**R

AR**OM**A
SO**LI**D
UN**DE**R
GR**EE**N
MA**RR**Y

Jammin'! (page 129)

Number Code: Presidents (page 130)

1. 14 + 4 − 13 = 5 N
  2 + 12 − 8 = 6 I
 20 + 2 − 9 = 13 X
 20 + 1 − 19 = 2 O
 12 + 9 − 16 = 5 N
2. 8 + 6 − 12 = 2 O
  5 + 5 − 6 = 4 B
 13 + 18 − 6 = 25 A
 17 + 9 − 6 = 20 M
 31 + 4 − 10 = 25 A
3. 13 + 2 − 14 = 1 C
 21 + 8 − 4 = 25 A
  6 + 20 − 7 = 19 R
 13 + 8 − 9 = 12 T
  4 + 21 − 7 = 18 E
 30 + 2 − 13 = 19 R

4. 13 + 11 − 5 = 19 R
 21 + 13 − 16 = 18 E
 17 + 14 − 6 = 25 A
 13 + 18 − 24 = 7 G
 16 + 17 − 8 = 25 A
 12 + 9 − 16 = 5 N
5. 5 + 15 − 8 = 12 T
  5 + 17 − 3 = 19 R
 12 + 12 − 3 = 21 U
  3 + 18 − 1 = 20 M
 18 + 8 − 1 = 25 A
  7 + 7 − 9 = 5 N

Answers

Farmer Maze (page 131)

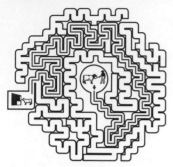

Fit It (page 132)

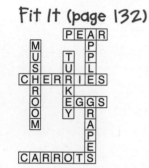

Toy Store (page 133)

America (pages 134–135)

Hoops (page 136)

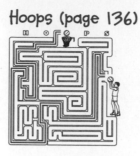

Theme Park (page 137)

Apple Fun (page 138)

Random Anagrams (page 139)

1. ate/tea; 2. bowl/blow; 3. wand/dawn;
4. aunt/tuna; 5. owl/low

Round 'em Up! (page 140)

There are 18 cows.

Paper Fold (page 141)

TOTAL

Flower Growth (page 141)

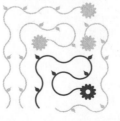

A Day at the Beach
(pages 142–143)

1. bathing suit, 2. boardwalk, 3. hermit crab,
4. jellyfish; 5. kite; 6. lotion; 7. sailboat; 8. sand
castle; 9. seagull; 10. seashell; 11. seaweed;
12. sunglasses; 13. surfboard; 14. towel;
15. umbrella; 16. waves

Rhyme Time (page 144)

1. cattle battle; 2. reel deal; 3. worm's germs;
4. each peach; 5. weaker speaker; 6. full bull;
7. camp champ; 8. noodle doodle; 9. strange
change; 10. ram exam; 11. brighter writer;
12. hates waits; 13. blue view; 14. thank Frank;
15. shady lady; 16. kinder reminder

Rapunzel (page 145)

Matching Blots (page 146)

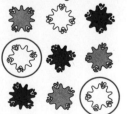

Vex-a-Gon (page 147)

Typewriter Error (page 147)

Canoe, Truck

Picture This (page 148)

Mutations (page 149)

A waist of paper!

1-2-3 (page 150)

Paper Fold (page 151)

TOPIC

Flippy Numbers (page 151)

$2 \times 36 = 12$

$2 \times 16 = 32$

Vex-a-Gon (page 152)

189

Answers

Word Ladder (page 152)

Answers may vary.

SOME, same, sane, mane, MANY

Theme Park (page 153)

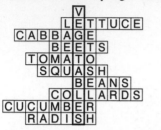

Rhyme Time (page 154)

1. slim limb; 2. drab crab; 3. red thread; 4. new clue; 5. space race; 6. guest test; 7. stone throne; 8. broke folk; 9. worse nurse; 10. boy's toys; 11. punk skunk; 12. mutt strut; 13. fair pair

Flower Power (page 155)

A. In B, the bottom flower is missing a petal; in C, the circle is filled in on the sides; in D, the top stem has lost its leaves.

Riddle in the Middle (page 156)

MA**Y**OR

QU**O**TE

YO**U**NG

ER**R**OR

OR**B**IT

ST**R**UM

DR**E**AM

ST**A**RE

TO**T**AL

AS**H**ES

Matching Blots (page 157)

Number Code: States (page 158)

1. $12 \div 2 = 6$ M
$33 \div 3 = 11$ A
$20 \div 4 = 5$ I
$40 \div 20 = 2$ N
$24 \div 6 = 4$ E
2. $30 \div 5 = 6$ M
$56 \div 7 = 8$ O
$14 \div 7 = 2$ N
$65 \div 5 = 13$ T
$99 \div 9 = 11$ A
$8 \div 4 = 2$ N
$44 \div 4 = 11$ A
3. $24 \div 4 = 6$ M
$88 \div 8 = 11$ A
$36 \div 4 = 9$ R
$36 \div 2 = 18$ Y
$75 \div 3 = 25$ L
$55 \div 5 = 11$ A
$26 \div 13 = 2$ N
$63 \div 3 = 21$ D

4. $48 \div 8 = 6$ M
$40 \div 8 = 5$ I
$35 \div 5 = 7$ C
$18 \div 6 = 3$ H
$50 \div 10 = 5$ I
$119 \div 7 = 17$ G
$77 \div 7 = 11$ A
$34 \div 17 = 2$ N
5. $60 \div 10 = 6$ M
$45 \div 9 = 5$ I
$36 \div 3 = 12$ S
$48 \div 4 = 12$ S
$72 \div 9 = 8$ O
$30 \div 2 = 15$ U
$72 \div 8 = 9$ R
$60 \div 12 = 5$ I

Flower Growth (page 159)

Vex-a-Gon (page 159)

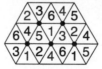

Flippy Numbers (page 160)

$8\boxed{1} \div \boxed{8} = \boxed{1}8$

$8\boxed{8} \div \boxed{8} = \boxed{1}\boxed{1}$

Chain Words (page 160)

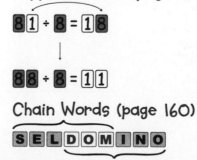

SELDOMINO

Halloween Costumes (page 161)

Theme Park (page 162)

```
RUNWAY
  WINDOWS
MOTOR
     PROP
 PILOT
 SEATS
 WINGS
  REARENGINE
```

Insect Anagrams (page 163)

Mosquito; dragonfly; butterfly; grasshopper;
ladybug; caterpillar; beetle; horsefly
Riddle answer: Moth ball

Find the Blocks (page 164)

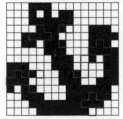

Fit It (page 165)

```
C        B
CARIPLANE
RD D      L
SAILBOAT L
  N O    O
  O A    N
ACES     S
  C A     C
  T U     L
  TORNADO O
  U       W
  SNOWMAN
```

Chain Words (page 166)

GOLFFRRFT

Word Math (page 166)

MAP + 80 (EIGHTY) − APE = M I G H T Y

Fishing (page 167)

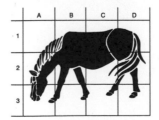

Math Class (pages 168–169)

```
PAL SUM ADD
USA IMA GAP
TABLE CARDS
   AS  SI
 PASTA MEAN
OOP ABS ROC
ZERO EQUAL
  PI US
CUBED ASHES
ONE EAR IVE
POT ADE DEW
```

Birds (page 170)

There are 25 total birds.

USA Anagrams (page 171)

1. California—Sacramento; 2. Texas—Austin;
3. Florida—Tallahassee; 4. New York—Albany;
5. Hawaii—Honolulu

Picture This (page 172)

Answers

Paper Fold (page 173)

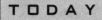

T O D A Y

Word Math (page 173)

PAW + LACE − W = PALACE

Fruits (page 174)

```
J Y N P P N B M D R A T S O C
R T Q M Q B A N A N A G L I O
P A P A Y A G Y E N L E W Y H
R U L B D R C R B O G X F R A
Q O L N K R J A N K O M R P
N M Q U I N C E A P D A T E P
E U U E R C I T B P E A R B L
K A B A Y H S N N O T N E
A N T E M E R E I X H A P A N
B N I R A P K R R A A G R I
W H O R T L E B E R R Y O C R
A E C Y O G D R R B Y J A L A
T G Z A N T A U S A E O G V T
A N K A E L C M R I L S O N C
C A T I D P A I B I M C O L E
Y R R E B L U M V D A M S O N
P O M E L O E E C D E N O E G
D H M D R U P E O L S Q K N L
```

192